MESSAGE OF THE FATHERS OF THE CHURCH

General Editor: Thomas Halton

Volume 18

MESSAGE OF THE FATHERS OF THE CHURCH

THE CHRISTIAN WAY OF LIFE

by

Francis X. Murphy, CSSR

Michael Glazier
Wilmington, Delaware

ABOUT THE AUTHOR

FRANCIS X. MURPHY, CSSR, patristic scholar and theologian, currently resides at St. Mary's in Annapolis, Maryland. Among his many publications are *A Monument to St. Jerome* and *Politics and the Early Christian*. A peritus of Vatican II, he is also widely known as an astute commentator on contemporary church affairs.

First published in 1986 by Michael Glazier, Inc.
1935 West Fourth Street, Wilmington, Delaware 19805.

Distributed outside U.S., Canada, Australia, and Philippines by Geoffrey Chapman, a division of Cassel Ltd., 1 Vincent Square, London SWIP 2PN.

Library of Congress Catalog Card Number: 85-45561
International Standard Book Number:
   Message of the Fathers of the Church series:
     (0-89453-312-6, Paper; 0-89453-340-1, Cloth)
THE CHRISTIAN WAY OF LIFE
   (0-89453-329-0, Paper)
   (0-89453-358-4, Cloth)

Cover design: Lillian Brulc

Typography by Debbie L. Farmer.

Printed in the United States.

Contents

Editor's Introduction

The *Message of the Fathers of the Church* is a companion series to The *Old Testament Message* and The *New Testament Message*. It was conceived and planned in the belief that Scripture and Tradition worked hand in hand in the formation of the thought, life and worship of the primitive Church. Such a series, it was felt, would be a most effective way of opening up what has become virtually a closed book to present-day readers, and might serve to stimulate a revival in interest in Patristic studies in step with the recent, gratifying resurgence in Scriptural studies.

The term "Fathers" is usually reserved for Christian writers marked by orthodoxy of doctrine, holiness of life, ecclesiastical approval and antiquity. "Antiquity" is generally understood to include writers down to Gregory the Great (+604) or Isidore of Seville (+636) in the West, and John Damascene (+749) in the East. In the present series, however, greater elasticity has been encouraged, and quotations from writers not noted for orthodoxy will sometimes be included in order to illustrate the evolution of the Message on particular doctrinal matters. Likewise, writers later than the mid-eighth century will sometimes be used to illustrate the continuity of tradition on matters like sacramental theology or liturgical practice.

An earnest attempt was made to select collaborators on a broad inter-disciplinary and inter-confessional basis, the chief consideration being to match scholars who could handle the Fathers in their original languages with subjects in which they had already demonstrated a special interest and competence. About the only editorial directive given to the selected contributors was that the Fathers, for the most part, should be allowed to speak for themselves and that

7

they should speak in readable, reliable modern English. Volumes on individual themes were considered more suitable than volumes devoted to individual Fathers, each theme, hopefully, contributing an important segment to the total mosaic of the Early Church, one, holy, catholic and apostolic. Each volume has an introductory essay outlining the historical and theological development of the theme, with the body of the work mainly occupied with liberal citations from the Fathers in modern English translation and a minimum of linking commentary. Short lists of Suggested Further Reading are included; but dense, scholarly footnotes were actively discouraged on the pragmatic grounds that such scholarly shorthand has other outlets and tends to lose all but the most relentlessly esoteric reader in a semi-popular series.

At the outset of his *Against Heresies* Irenaeus of Lyons warns his readers "not to expect from me any display of rhetoric, which I have never learned, or any excellence of composition, which I have never practised, or any beauty or persuasiveness of style, to which I make no pretensions." Similarly, modest disclaimers can be found in many of the Greek and Latin Fathers and all too often, unfortunately, they have been taken at their word by an uninterested world. In fact, however, they were often highly educated products of the best rhetorical schools of their day in the Roman Empire, and what they have to say is often as much a lesson in literary and cultural, as well as in spiritual, edification.

St. Augustine, in *The City of God* (19.7), has interesting reflections on the need for a common language in an expanding world community; without a common language a man is more at home with his dog than with a foreigner as far as intercommunication goes, even in the Roman Empire, which imposes on the nations it conquers the yoke of both law and language with a resultant abundance of interpreters. It is hoped that in the present world of continuing language barriers the contributors to this series will prove opportune interpreters of the perennial Christian message.

Thomas Halton

Preface

This monograph on the Patristic Ethic is not intended as a taxative enumeration of the moral thinking of the early church Fathers. Nor is it intended as a systematic study of their ethical perspective. It is rather an exemplification of these churchmen in their everyday activities reacting to the need for information and guidance expressed by their people who were in search of the authentic Christian way of life. Justification for this approach is supplied by the fact that, with exceptions, the church fathers did not attempt to systematize their moral teaching. Rather their exhortations to virtue and to a way of life inserted in the church as the body of Christ arose from a constant meditation on the Scriptures. It received its formulation in homilies and tracts reflecting the immediate needs of the Christian's daily awareness.

The material collected here represents the substance of lectures delivered at the Academia Alfonsiana in Rome, and embodied in books and articles beginning with "The Background to a History of Patristic Moral Thought," in *Studia Moralia* 1 (Rome, 1963) pp. 48-85; *Moral Teaching of the Primitive Church* (New York: Newman, 1968); and a series of papers on Tertullian, Rufinus of Aquileia, Basil, Hilary of Poitiers, and John Chrysostom read at Patristic Congresses in Oxford from 1963 to 1979 and published in *Studia Patristica* (Berlin).

The translations are mainly my own with a generous assist from the standard English versions in *The Fathers of the Church, Ancient Christian Writers, Nicene* and *Post Nicene Fathers,* the *Loeb* series, and individual versions of particular fathers.

Special thanks is due to Michael Glazier and Professor Thomas Halton for inviting me to contribute this volume to the *Message of the Fathers of the Church;* and particular gratitude is due to Eileen Carzo for her patience as editor in dealing with a dilatory author; and to Marie Porter for invaluable assistance in deciphering, rearranging and typing the manuscript.

St. Mary's, Annapolis
October 15, 1985.

Introduction

In the preface to his French edition of Samuel Pufendorf's *Of the Law of Nature and of Nations*, the eighteenth century Protestant jurist, Jean Barbeyrac, suggested that almost all the Fathers of the first six centuries had fallen into the grossest errors on the subject of morals. Barbeyrac was but echoing what had become a commonplace of post-Reformation, anti-Catholic polemic. Thus, some ten years later, Barbeyrac was astonished to find himself the primary target of Dom Remy Ceillier's *Apology for the Moral Teaching of the Fathers*. Eventually in his own *Treatise on the Moral of the Church Fathers*, Barbeyrac supplied a brisk counter-attack on what he termed Dom Ceillier's fanatical defense of the Catholic position on tradition in its ethical teaching.

Barbeyrac documents his original charge by citing numerous patristic moral opinions that he considers gravely erroneous or in extremely poor taste. He charges Clement of Alexandria, for example, with a vain display of learning; and accuses him, together with Tertullian, Augustine and Jerome, with offending against propriety in the frankness with which they discuss the sexual aspects of marriage.

The difficulty with this hypercritical approach to the moral thought of the early Christian churchmen is that it reflects a reading of the Fathers that is at once out of context and usually out of humor. It takes little notice of the social, philosophic and religious milieu in which the patristic moral had been produced. Five centuries earlier Thomas Aquinas had supplied a nuanced criticism of many moral opinions of the early churchmen, but he did so with the purpose of correcting and improving upon what they had accomplished.

Insofar as the social and historical milieu of the patristic period was concerned, Thomas Aquinas suffered from a greater disadvantage than that of the eighteenth century scholars. Yet, despite his rigid, scholastic approach, Thomas considered the Fathers neither beyond criticism with Ceillier nor largely unreasonable with Barbeyrac. For he did have some idea of the difficulties that had been encountered by the early Christian churchmen in fusing the Judeo-Christian faith and moral values with the ethical accomplishments of the Hellenistic and Oriental cultures of their day. Recognizing the efforts made by the patristic moralists to discuss human nature on the basis of reason employed within a biblical context, Thomas Aquinas found in the patristic elaboration of Christ's moral teaching an authentic if, at times, incomplete expression of the Christian way of life.

Contemporary interest in a renewal of the Church's moral teaching is calling for both an updating in its social, political and psychological orientation and its reintegration in a wider theological perspective. In this endeavor both inspiration and direction are being sought through a renewed reading of the scriptures — both the Old and New Testaments — and the elaboration of Christ's teaching as perceived by the early church thinkers and teachers.

It would be unrealistic to seek a truly organic development in the moral thinking of the early churchmen, or to impose on the patristic moral endeavor, generally, or on the thinking of a particular Father, the categories or systematic schematization of a later age, particularly that of the scholastic period, or of contemporary manuals of ethics or moral theology. Nevertheless, there is a discernible pattern that is woven through their exhortatory and exegetical works and that gives substance and direction to their ethical preaching. Actually, there is discernible a considerable evolution and a progressive refining of ethical teaching from the first post-apostolic moral catechesis in the *Didache* or Teaching of the Apostles and the *Letter of Pseudo Barnabas* to the specifically moral treatises of Ambrose and Augustine in the west and the catechetical exhortations of a John Chrysostom and a Maximus the Confessor in the east.

Studies dealing with the moral teaching of the Old and New Testaments are comparatively plentiful. Their end result, generally speaking, is the conclusion that the moral teaching of Christ as recorded in the Gospels and diffused through the oral preaching and the documents of the New Testament was a reanimation of the basic Jewish moral wisdom, which had been impregnated by contact with Hellenic thought primarily in the Jewish diaspora several centuries earlier, and colored by the ascetical tendencies of the Essenes or the devotees of Qumran.

What was truly original in Christ's moral teaching was its unequivocally spiritual orientation, and the absolute authority with which he invested his ethical commandments. Thus, the substance of the Sermon on the Mount and the two commandments of love of God and love of neighbor can be found literally in the Old Testament, specifically in Leviticus and Deuteronomy. But his claim to be the Son of God, his insistence on the fact that he was "the way, the truth and the life," his invitation to penance and the imitation of his humility and patience, and his enunciation of his ethical requirements in an eschatological perspective gave Christ's doctrines a revolutionary aspect. It was in this guise that the Christian moral teaching was handed on to the primitive communities of the first century.

There is a striking similarity between the moral thunderings of the ancient Jewish prophets, such as Isaiah and Amos, and the ethical injunctions in Hesiod's *Work and Days*, in Solon, and the earlier Greek philosophers. This fact, particularly in the teaching of Socrates and Plato, did not escape the early Christian Fathers, beginning with Justin Martyr and Clement of Alexandria. The latter was primarily influenced by the Jewish sage, Philo of Alexandria (20 BC to 50 AD), who had made a successful effort to bridge the Hebrew and Hellenic cultures. This infiltration of Hellenic elements into Judaic thought began with the Sapiential literature of the Old Testament. While there is a fundamental difference between the basic ideology of the later pagan moralists, particularly the Stoics, and the Judeo-Christian moral doctrine, the technique of preaching and the inculcation of virtue in actual practice were all but identical in the two cultures.

The later pagan philosophers, from Plutarch and Cicero to Seneca and Marcus Aurelius, reflecting in good part Aristotle's *Nichomachean Ethics*, cultivated a self-contained, non-religious, logically coherent system of ethics based on the nature of man, and on a rational analysis of his reaction to daily experience. Recognizing his inner self as fundamentally reasonable, man desired to direct his activities in an orderly fashion by mastering his passions, eliminating vice, and freeing himself from baser preoccupations.

The early Christian propagandists employed the techniques used by the wandering philosophers and moralists, particularly the Stoics, Epicureans, and Pythagoreans, who went from town to town throughout the Roman Empire, laying down a strict code of moral conduct whose aim was a reasonable approach to the problems of daily life. There were numerous instances in which both the Jewish and the Stoic moral teaching were in agreement. Hence, it was but normal that they would have employed similar methods in outlining behaviour patterns.

Describing the elements of a liberal education, the Roman biographer and Stoic, Plutarch, maintained: "With wisdom and through her, it is given to know the beautiful and the shameful, the just and unjust; what to accept and what should be avoided ... Wisdom prescribes reverence for the gods, honor for parents, respect for elders, obedience to the laws, submission to the magistrates, love for friends, wise and reserved conduct with women, the cherishing of children, and that one should never get incensed with slaves" (*On a Liberal Education*, 10).

Both Plato and Aristotle had developed the ethical teaching of Greek philosophy on the premise that the wise man was capable of controlling his inner drives by the practice of virtue. In so doing they distinguished between man's inner consciousness and the emotions and passions in his rational, irascible, and concupiscible appetites. This structural concept became the common conviction of the moral philosophers, and was taken over by the church Fathers once they began to give a reasonable explanation for their inculcation of ethical values. In general, the earlier churchmen made no attempt to analyze the nature of virtue as a human experience or endeavor, nor did they distinguish between the intellectual and the moral virtues. All formed an integrated pattern of the good life, and where the conclusions of right reason had been codified in law (*nomos*), obedience to the law, both divine and human, was considered virtuous.

The Jewish and Christian ethic, on the other hand, was not self-contained or self-justifying. It had as its basis the Word of God contained in the Scriptures. As its end or purpose, it proclaimed obedience to, and union with, a transcendent Being. But even here, there were elements in both the Platonic and Aristotelian teaching that resembled the Judeo-Christian religious foundations of the practice of virtue. Plato in the *Laws* spoke of the right *paideia* or educational practice inculcated by the divinity as its ultimate source. Aristotle constructed his ethics on the basis of a "natural theology." In the end, for both the pagan and the Judeo-Christian ethic, God was the pedagogue of the universe.

What the Hellenic culture contributed to orthodox Christian theology was, for the most part, a vocabulary and a new mode of expressing notions that had long formed part of the later Judaic tradition. In the sphere of ethics, the Stoic and Platonic ideas helped to clarify the anthropology and the rational basis by which the Christian moral teaching was elucidated. But this explicit influence is comparatively late; it comes with the Apologists and the Fathers of the late second century. Meanwhile, the Judeo-Christian theology was in possession. While the Hellenistic ideals of the Stoics and Neoplatonists gave an immediately more rational and more mystical turn to the Christian moral thought, they did not supply any of the fundamental tenets of the basic Christian belief.

What modern investigation has ascertained is the fact that the earliest exponents of the Christian religion had worked out a distinctive way of presenting the fundamental convictions of their faith in a formula which they called the proclamation or *kerygma.* It was the equivalent of the Hellenic protreptic or invitational discourse. The Christian preacher thought of himself as an announcer or herald of very important news. He recounted the life and work of Jesus Christ in brief form, demonstrating that in Christ's worldly conflicts, his sufferings, death and resurrection, the divinely guided history of Israel had reached its climax. God himself had now personally intervened in the history of mankind to inaugurate His kingdom upon earth.

The preacher then sought to convince his hearers that they were now confronted by God Himself as represented in His kingdom, which was the new Christian community or church; that they stood liable to His judgment, which was immediate and inescapable. They had only to accept His invitation to embark on a new way of life, wherein, through God's mercy, they would be unburdened of past delinquencies, and have the opportunity of enjoying a new and close relationship with God, in Christ Jesus, dead and risen from the dead. The names of those who accepted this message were inscribed in the new community or Church. They were given instruction in moral principles and sanctifying practices that were essential to the Christian way of life.

This latter course in moral behavior was distinctive from the proclamation of the Gospel as such. It was an immediate preparation for the reception of Baptism, and included prayer and fasting by way of driving out evil spirits. This order of presenting the new Christian fact — first the *kerygma* or announcement, then the *didache,* or moral teaching on an eschatological background — seems to have been characteristic of all the primitive preaching. As such, it was a direct outgrowth of the Jewish tradition within which Christianity arose. For both the Decalogue and the grand structure of the Law or *Torah* begin with a statement of divine fact: "I am the Lord thy God, Who brought thee out of the land of Egypt!" This statement was supported by an intertwining of historical events portraying God's providence and care for His People. On this background, the ethical requirements or commandments of the Law are imposed.

The Christian moral teaching thus inherited a dynamic sense of God's presence in the form of divine Wisdom that permeated creation, and sanctified the man who devoted himself to the cultivation of God's law or the *Torah*. In the Jewish Law was embodied the *derek tebunot*, or divine insight, which led a man to identify the way of wisdom (*hokmah*) with the right conduct of life. The rabbis had developed this doctrine in a moral and spiritual sense, insisting that the *shekinah* or divine presence inhabited only the hearts of the humble, giving them wisdom. Thus, evil inclinations could be overcome by the contemplation of the *Torah*, which made the wise man gentle, kind and pious.

St. Paul identified this rabbinic way of wisdom with the imitation of Christ who is the "power of God, the wisdom of God." In accepting Christ as Lord, the new Christian was engrafted into the assembly or Church (*ecclesia*), which, as the body of Christ, was likewise the way of wisdom leading to salvation. This teaching is developed in two differing but mutually dependent traditions among the earlier churchmen. In the later New Testament documents and among the post-apostolic Fathers, it is rabbinic, homiletic tradition that prevails. Wisdom is the result of the acceptance of Christ as the way, the truth, and the life. It is, thus, the means of sanctification.

With the apologists of the second century, on the other hand, Christ and wisdom are identical. In the attempt to demonstrate the divinity of Jesus as the Lord and Saviour, he is explicitly identified with the *logos* as *sophia* or Wisdom incarnate.

It is with the second-century churchmen, likewise, that the Hellenistic concept of wisdom or *sophia* formally enters into the Christian theological development. The Septuagint translation of the hebraic *hokmah* by the Greek *sophia* or wisdom is more a virtue than a philosophical concept. It is used of one who "practised what he preached." In later usage it retained the notion of both superior knowledge and right conduct. Plato speaks of the wise man who "becomes like god, by being just and holy," and Plotinus speaks of *wisdom* as the life of the soul illumined from within. In both Virgil and Cicero the Latin *sapientia* is used in this virtue-implied context.

It was but natural that the primitive Christian catechesis should have developed within the framework of the Jewish manner of indoctrinating proselytes. Basic to this latter procedure were the rules laid down for baptism, circumcision and sacrifice to be followed in the initiation of the pagan convert to Judaism. When, then, the crisis caused by the dispute over the manner of inducting pagan converts into the Christian community as recorded in the *Acts of the Apostles* was settled by the meeting of Apostles at Jerusalem in 51 AD, it was decided that the new convert to Christianity should be baptized, but then, in place of circumcision and sacrifice, he should be constrained to forswear idolatry, murder and shameful things (*porneia*). This basic procedure can be seen as the substratum of the first and second Epistles to the Thessalonians and in the first Epistle of Peter. What is more, it is located in an eschatological setting, wherein the newly baptized Christians are urged to be steadfast in persecution, awaiting the second coming of Christ. They are further assured that as members of the Church, that is the body of Christ, they are the children of Light, employing our Lord's own expression; that therefore they are to avoid the doings of darkness: evil conduct, drunkenness and excess, as defined by Christ.

In 1 Thessalonians, St. Paul contrasted night as the time for revelry and sleep, with the day which calls for wakefulness and sobriety. He advises his Christians that as children of the light and of the day they have a new status; they are living in a new order in which a purposeful approach to life and self-discipline is required.

The first Epistle of Peter echoes this teaching. It singles

out, among the lusts to be avoided, drunkenness as particularly characteristic of the life of death led before their conversion. This passage follows on what has been described as
Peter's baptismal teaching. There is a similar passage in the
Epistle to the Romans. Finally, an absolute emphasis was
placed on the practice of humility and mutual charity as
required for the proper ordering of the Christian way of life
within the community.

Throughout the early church documents there is thus an
emphasis on the positive, practical ordinances of moral
conduct in reference to faith and love of God, in the Christian's personal obligations within the Church, in family life,
and in the relations of masters and slaves, as well as in the
loyalty and obedience owed to civil authorities. What is
clear is the fact that in these adaptations of the Law of Christ
to the exigencies of daily life in the Roman Empire of the
first century AD, the Christian catechists were conscious of
the presence within their community and selves of a higher,
supernatural reality whence sprang these obligations.

At the same time, it was in this development of the
Christian message as a dynamic force in contact with the
world about it that the so-called Hellenistic elements eventually forced themselves into the Christian scheme of things
without, however, causing any essential modification of the
original message of Christ. In actual fact, between the New
Testament writings and the appearance of the earliest post-
apostolic documents, the development of doctrinal and
moral thought in the various communities of the primitive
Church was brought about by what has been designated as
the theology of Judeo-Christianity. In the sphere of ethics,
the Stoic and Platonic ideas did help to clarify the anthropology and the rational basis upon which the Christian
moral teaching was explained. But this explicit influence is
comparatively late; it is introduced with the Apologists and
fathers of the late second century. By that time, the Judeo-
Christian theology was in possession. And while the Hellenistic ideas introduced an immediately more rational and
more mystical turn to Christian thought, they did not
supply any of the fundamental tenets of that belief.

Chapter One

The Early Christian Ethic

Between the death of Christ and that of the last apostle, there is a gap of some sixty years. During that interval, the Church spread from Jerusalem and Palestine to Syria, Egypt, Asia Minor, Greece and Rome. Although in the Gospels the activities of Jesus are portrayed mostly in rural areas, the spread of early Christianity seems to have been mainly an urban development. The apostles and disciples first approached their Jewish brethren in the synagogues of the larger cities of the empire - Antioch, Alexandria, Corinth, Athens and Rome. Upon rejection by their Jewish contemporaries, they turned to interested gentiles. There seems to have been no distinction of class among the early converts. Rich and poor, slave and freedmen were welcomed into the new communities whose place of assembly were in the homes of the fairly well-to-do.

Under these circumstances, the New Testament teaching gave rise to a theological ethic that is reflected immediately in the so-called post-apostolic documents in the form of homiletic and epistolarly treatises whose substance is the moral catechesis or instruction. They include the *Didache* or Teaching of the Apostles, the *Letter of the Ps. Barnabas*, the *Letter of Clement of Rome*, the *Pastor Hermas*, the *Epistles of Ignatius of Antioch* and the *Letter of Polycarp*. Though it is impossible to date these documents with precision or to trace their provenance, from the final version of the *Didache* to the *Pastor Hermas*, they cover a period of fifty or more years, roughly from A.D. 95 to 145 or so.

Of these documents, the *Letter of Clement* reflects the ecclesial situation in two established Christian communities - Rome and Corinth - towards the end of the first century. It is certain that the Didache, at least in its final form, represents a standardized Jewish moral treatise with strong Christian interpolations that was handed down, probably in the Church of Syria, in the decades before the end of the first century. The *Letter of the Ps. Barnabas* can, with some reason, be considered of Egyptian origin, probably the product of an Alexandrian community about A.D. 115. The *Letters of Ignatius* and that of *Polycarp* are the products of the Christian assembly in Antioch of Syria, while the *Pastor Hermas* returns us to the Roman scene *circa* 145 A.D.

Despite etiological uncertainties, these texts present an approximation of the state of the Christian moral thinking in four main centers of the primitive church - Rome, Corinth, Antioch and Alexandria. Hence, they witness to the first steps of the early Christian ethical development.

The second-century world and our own are immensely different in the organization of business, commerce, transportation, recreation, and even household and other facilities of convenience. At the same time, however, the ancient world lacked none of these elements as the archeological remains of cities like Ostia and Pompeii amply attest. Ancient man moved at a snail's pace compared to turbojet flying, yet he traveled. Pilgrimages were made frequently both by pagans and Christians; Christ and the apostles were continually traveling through Palestine. Likewise in the big cities, such as Rome and Alexandria, people lived in apartment houses of four and five stories; they had plumbing and great public baths. They had circuses and theaters, and the citizens met and amused themselves in the public squares where they could frequently attend the harangues of itinerant philosophers, such as the Stoics or Epicureans, as well as the performances of minstrels and mountebanks. Commerce was well organized and stable; merchants operated stores and traveling salesmen plied their wares. Life in both large urban centers and villages with its complications and temptations did resemble life today. The danger of corruption was equally great, if not more so, since the police and other public safety factors were nowhere as well organized as they are today. The admonitions of the Christian moral teacher were, therefore, well taken whether he was addressing an audience in a synagogue in Alexandria, or a smaller house group in a town or village. They have immediate meaning for us nowadays, despite the apparent sophistication of our lives and interests.

The Didache or Teaching of the Twelve Apostles

The tract called the *Didache*, or *Teaching of the Twelve Apostles*, was discovered by the Orthodox Metropolitan Bishop Byrennios at Constantinople in 1873, and is recognized as one of the earliest non-biblical documents of the Christian Church. It professes to be an instruction based on the sayings of the Lord as presented by the twelve apostles to pagans who desired to become Christians.

Neither the true title nor the date of composition of this document is known. However, it is certain that the tract represents an originally Jewish instruction formulary that was used as a basis for Christian teaching during the first century A.D. The Christian elements, notably those describing baptism and the celebration of the eucharist, are primitive. While many of the statements seem to reflect quotations from the gospels of Matthew and Luke (without direct dependence, however), there is the possibility that they were interpolations made at a much later date.

The teachings regarding the *Two Ways*, the love of God and of neighbor, the golden rule, fasting and prayer, the requirements of hospitality, and the support of prophets and itinerant missionaries, represent authentic Jewish ethical doctrine. But scholars concede that it is a Christian document, though even the directions regarding baptism and the eucharistic or thanksgiving repast, with its messianic yearning, could be strictly Jewish. In itself the document is mainly a moral treatise and testifies to the deep religious conviction of the early Christian community.

> Two ways there are, one of life and one of death, and there is a great difference between the two ways. 1.2. The way of life is this: First, love the God who made you; then, love your neighbor as yourself. Do not do to another what you do not wish to be done to you. . . . *Didache* 1,2[1]

This exhortation is buttressed by a series of practial applications drawn directly from the Gospels:

> Bless those who curse you and pray for your enemies; even fast for those who persecute you. For what thanks should you have if you love those who love you? Do not the pagans do as much? Love those who hate you. In fact you should have no enemy. *Didache* 3[2]

> My child, shun evil of any kind and everything resembling it. Do not be prone to anger, for anger leads to murder. Do not be fanatical, nor quarrelsome, nor hottempered; for all these things beget murder. My child, do not be lustful, for lust leads to fornication. Do not be foul mouthed or give free rein to your eyes; for all these things beget adultery. My child, do not be an auger, because it leads to idolatry. Do not be an enchanter; nor an astrologer, nor an expiator, and do not wish to see these things; for they all beget idolatry. My child do not be a liar, for

[1]SC 248, 140-142
[2]SC 248, 142-144

lying leads to theft. Do not be a lover of money, or a vain pretender. All these things beget thievery. My child, do not be a grumbler, because it leads to blashemy; or self-willed, or evil-minded. All these things beget blasphemy.

Didache 3[3]

The technique employed as a method of instruction in which the father addressed his son: "My child, shun evil . . . do not . . ." is an ancient device for handing on wisdom. It reflects the teaching method of Exodus (20:1-17) and Deuteronomy (5:6-21) as well as of the later Psalms, Ecclesiasticus (ch. 24), and Widsom, and was used by the Jewish theologian, Philo of Alexandria. It was employed also in giving a commentary on the decalog or Ten Commandments, after the fashion of the catalog of virtues and vices popular in both Hellenistic and Jewish ethical teaching.

The principal warnings are against the apparently minor vices of superstition, because they so easily led to such major crimes as homicide, lust, and idolatry. The condemnation of scanning the future through examining the entrails, or the flight of birds, or of participation in the expiatory ceremonies of the pagan religions, was based on a practical, moral psychology. These warnings recall Christ's insistence on keeping "the least of these commandments" (Mt. 5:19). Superstitious and idolatrous practices were a great temptation for Jews and Christians under the impulse of the Roman religious practices that were part of the everyday civic life. Besides, the sins of fornication and idolatry were specifically ruled against in the so-called Jerusalem decrees (Acts 15:28; 21:25).

> On the contrary be gentle for the gentle will inherit the land . . . . 4.5. Do not be one who opens his hands to receive, but shuts them when it comes to giving. If you have means at your disposal, pay a ransom for your sins. Do not hesitate to give, and do not give in a grumbling

[3]SC 248, 152-154

mood. You will find out who is the good rewarder. Do not turn away from the needy; rather, share everything with your brother, and do not say: It is my property. If you are sharers in what is imperishable, how much more so in the things that perish! *Didache* 3,2-4, 5[4]

The advice to cultivate the virtue of gentleness pertains to the so-called Instruction for the Poor that was a popular manner of preaching among the Jewish sages and rabbis, while the exhortations regarding almsgiving reflect the frequent insistence on this practice in Tobias (4:7-11), Proverbs (19:17) and Ecclesiasticus (3:30; 4:1-6). There seems to be a gradation between the occasional almsgiver (5), the one who regularly bestows charity (6), and the suggestion that one in comfortable means should "share everything with his brother" after the fashion of the *koinonia* or community-sharing described in Acts (2:4; 4:32), which seems to have been more or less a common custom among the Jewish poor. The reference to "what is imperishable" means, of course, the goods of the faith, and brings in the note of the messianic hope accomplished in Christ's resurrection.

Do not withdraw your hand from your son or your daughter, but from their youth teach them the fear of God. Do not, when embittered, give orders to your slaves, male or female, for they have hope in the *same* God; otherwise, they might lose the fear of God who is the master of both of you. He is surely not coming to call with an eye to rank, or station in life; no, He comes to those whom the Spirit has prepared. But you, slaves, be submissive to your masters as to God's image ... In church confess your sins, and do not come to prayer with a guilty conscience.
Such is the Way of Life. *Didache* 4, 9[5]

---

[4]SC 248, 154-160
[5]SC 248, 162-166

The type of instruction which the father was specifically encouraged to give to his growing son and daughter is probably that contained in chapter 3:1-6, and is based on Deuteronomy (6:7; 11:19). The need for this observation rose from the fact that, generally speaking, the mother was considered in charge of the household and children, but as the period of youth continued to the age of twenty, the father's authority had to be brought to bear.

The humane treatment of slaves here cited was based on religious motives as well as prudence in keeping with the gentleness praised earlier (3:7). The concurrent admonition to the slave that he should see the image of God in his master indicates a familiarity between servants and masters that was proper to the Jewish household, and was certainly adopted by the Christians. This same teaching is repeated almost *verbatim* in the *Pseudo-Barnabas* (19:7). The reminder that the Lord is no respecter of persons is paralleled in Luke (22:24-27). The whole instruction has similarities with St. Paul's teaching in Ephesians (6:4-9) and Colossians (22:24-27), particularly where he cautions parents against provoking their children to rebellion by too great rigidity. The command to confess one's sins before the assembly or church, and not to pray with a bad conscience, seems to reflect older Jewish practices as in the Psalms (32:1-5; 41:5; 51).

The attitude of the primitive Church toward slavery is bound to puzzle the modern reader. Actually only the Stoics made any great attempt to abolish the institution and they were considered irrational and out of touch with reality. St. Paul and 1 Peter consider the problem settled when they tell the early Christians that in God's sight all men are equal. Considering the social and economic organization of society at the time, it seemed inconceivable to their contemporaries that life, or business, or even politics could be pursued if the services performed by slaves were abolished. This idea persisted in some parts of the United States until the end of the 19th century.

The early Church told slaves to honor their masters as representing God's will for them. It told the masters to care for their slaves as members or even children of their own household. Many pagans so treated their slaves; hence, the Christian should be even more conscientious, since they knew that Christ on the last day would be a strict judge in this matter. Actually in a good household, slaves lived comparatively well; they had an immunity from taxes and many dangers of life that many free men did not enjoy. However, slavery was a great evil; so great that it took 1,900 years to be completely abolished.

> The Way of Death is this: First of all it is wicked and altogether accursed ... It is the way of persecutors of the good, haters of the truth ... of men who have no heart for the poor, are not concerned about the oppressed, do not know their Maker ... of men who ... act as counsels for the rich, are unjust judges of the poor - in a word, of men steeped in sin. Children, may you be preserved from all this.
>
> 6.1. See that no man leads you astray from our Way of the Teaching, since any other teaching takes you away from God. Surely, if you are able to bear the Lord's yoke in its entirety, you will be perfect; if you are not able, then do what you can ... *Didache* 5,1-6,1[6]

The list of vices here detailed also seems to be in keeping with Old Testament teaching, but they can be paralleled all through the New Testament as well. The emphasis on the misuse of the poor and oppressed seems to confirm the fact that the teacher was addressing a middle or upper class audience; his remarks about those serving as advocates for the rich calls to mind Christ's condemnation of the legalisms of the Pharisees. There is here, too, a compassion for human weakness that harks back to the cautions in favor of gentleness, particularly in the suggestion that they who cannot keep the Law (of Christ, presumably) perfectly, should do as much as they can.

[6]SC 248, 166-168

The author is obviously addressing a group of believers who assembled regularly in the synagogue, or a house, or church for religious service. His form indicates that they are of a pious cast of mind, but that they are engaged in the ordinary occupations of everyday life. They are thus exposed to the evil talk and actions pursued by outsiders in business, in legal cases, in plain living. While warning against contamination, he does not suggest that his hearers cut themselves off from this world. Rather he wants to strengthen their resolutions to live uncontaminated lives and to demonstrate the presence of God's goodness among them.

> 7. Accordingly when an itinerant preacher teaches you all that has just been said, welcome him ... Upon his arrival, every apostle must be welcomed as the Lord: but he must not stay except one day. In case of necessity, however, he may stay another day; but if he stays three days, he is a false prophet. At his departure the apostle must receive nothing except food to last till the next night's lodging. If he asks for money, he is a false prophet ... Not everyone speaking in ecstasy is a prophet, except he has the ways of the Lord about him ... No prophet who in an ecstasy orders the table spread, should partake of it; otherwise he is a false prophet. Any prophet that teaches the truth, yet does not live up to his teaching , is a false prophet. 12.1. Anyone coming in the name of the Lord must be welcomed; but after that, test him and find out. You will use your discretion either for or against him. If the arrival is a transient visitor, assist him as much as you can; but he may not stay with you more than two days, or if necessary, three. If he intends to settle among you, then in case he is a craftsman, let him work for his living. If he has no trade or craft, use your judgment in providing for him, so that a follower of Christ will not live idle in your midst. But if he is not satisfied with your arrangements, he is trading on Christ. *Didache* 11, 1-12, 5[7]

[7]SC 248, 182-188

The Didachist distinguishes between apostles, prophets, and doctors, as he lays down guidance for dealing with itinerant preachers and teachers. What he makes plain in chapters 11-14 is that while the virtues of hospitality and of docility to the Spirit of God are highly praiseworthy, the householder should not be put upon foolishly. Since inns or hostels were all but non-existent outside the populous cities, and even there they presented great dangers, hospitality was an essential function of ancient civilized life. But, as appears from St. Paul's frequent insistence on supporting himself, the abuse of this service was great. Hence, the detailed instruction as to judging the reliability of the prophet, while urging great caution lest an authentic prophecy be misjudged. The discernment of spirits, or the evaluation of true spiritual testimony, became an issue in the early church: here the problem is merely hinted at, but there is plain speech in regard to the idle drifter anxious to abuse hospitality.

> Elect for yourselves bishops and deacons, men who are in honor to the Lord, of gentle disposition, not attached to money, honest and well-tried. For they too render you the sacred service of the prophets and teachers . . . Furthermore, correct one another, not in anger, but in composure, as you have it in the gospel; and when anyone offends his neighbor, let no one speak with him . . . until he has made amends.
>
> Watch over your life; your lamps must not go out, nor your loins be ungirded; on the contrary be ready . . . assemble in large numbers, intent upon what concerns your souls. Surely, of no use will your lifelong faith be, if you are not perfected in the end of time . . . *Didache* 15, 1-16,2[8]

After advising about the election of worthy bishops and deacons for the community, and re-enforcing the mandate

[8]SC 248, 192-194

of fraternal charity, the instruction closes with a prophetic warning about the rise of false prophets and the coming persecutions. Its overall message, however, sounds the note of a hope-giving eschatology.

The Letter of the Pseudo-Barnabas

The *Letter of the Pseudo-Barnabas* is a theological tract like the *Didache*. It is addressed to a convert group, but the unknown author is much more sophisticated than the Didachist. The text is found in the 4th century Codex Sinaiticus immediately after the canonical documents of the New Testament, and was considered by some early churchmen as part of the inspired word of God. It was thus attributed to the disciple, Barnabas, but its real author is unknown. It was probably written in the fourth decade of the 2nd century, for it refers to the destruction of the Jewish temple in Jerusalem, probably under the Emperor Hadrian (d. A.D. 135). It was quoted or used by the Shepherd of Hermas, Justin Martyr, Irenaeus, Clement of Alexandria, and Origen.

The letter form is a literary genre frequently used to express doctrinal instruction. While the writer betrays a rabbinic education, he is a well-instructed Christian, and proclaims the fact that Jesus Christ appeared in the flesh and shed his blood for our salvation (5). Through the incarnation and passion of Christ which were foretold by the prophets, we are redeemed from our sins (6).

The principal thesis of the letter, however, is directed toward proving that the Jews never really understood the meaning of the old Law and its ceremonies, and that their heritage has been taken over by the Christians, who now understand that the circumcision prescribed to Abraham was in reality a mystery looking forward to Jesus (9). The Jewish rulings concerning food and cermonies, likewise, should not have been understood literally. They conveyed a strictly spiritual lesson (10). Now God has enlightened the Christians concerning the water of baptism (11) and the prefiguring of the cross of Christ in Jewish history (12).

Jesus Christ is our true mediator (13), and the Sabbath is the
"day of eternity," the eighth day which the Christians, by
their Sunday service, celebrate in anticipation of the second
coming of the Lord (15). The true worship of God does not
take place in the Temple, but in our hearts, God's spiritual
temple. This will continue until the building up of Christ's
temple in its final splendor (16).

> We must carefully study the present situation and find
> out the means of our salvation. Hence let us shun abso-
> lutely every kind of evil-doing, or evil-doing will get the
> better of us. Let us scorn the error of the present time, and
> we shall be loved in the time to come. Do not indulge our
> natural appetites; otherwise they will without let or hin-
> drance conform to the ways of sinners and reprobates,
> and we shall be just like them ... my chief concern is to
> write as your humble friend, as becomes one who is
> anxious that we should sacrifice nothing of what we
> possess. Let us, then, be on guard in these days. Surely of
> no use will be the whole span of our lifelong faith if we do
> not, here and now, in this era of lawlessness, and amidst
> the seductions yet to come, take a firm stand as becomes
> the children of God ... Do not shut yourselves up and
> court solitude as though your justification were already
> assured.
>
> On the contrary, attend the common meetings, and join
> in discussing what contributes to the common good ...
> The Lord will judge the world without partiality. Eve-
> ryone will be rewarded according to his conduct: if one is
> good, his holiness will prepare the way for him; if one is
> wicked, the wages of his wickedness are in store for him.
> *Letter of Barnabas* 4 [9]

The *Letter of the Pseudo-Barnabas* is primarily an ethical
instruction. As such, it concentrates on the actual situation
in which the new Christian is to lead his life. Like Ignatius of

[9]SC 172, 92-102

Antioch in his *Letter to Polycarp* (ch. 3), and the new *Pastoral Constitution on the Church in the Modern World* (Prologue), the author tells his audience: "Read the signs of the times." The author describes the Christian way of life against a background of Christ's passion, death, and resurrection. Barnabas insists on the "hope of life eternal," as the beginning and end of the Christian's faith. This is anchored in the pursuit of holiness that brings with it love and genuine happiness in God's judgment (1:6).

To achieve this holiness, the Christian must keep himself from the sinfulness and lawlessness characteristic of the world about him. The author seems to be referring to the temptation of converts from Judaism to return to the old observances under the impulse of the sect of Hebrew zealots who tried to rebuild the Temple of Jerusalem.

> As to what Moses said: you shall eat neither swine, nor eagle ... nor fish without scales. These are properly understood as three moral principles ... Speaking of swine he meant, do not associate with people who resemble swine: who forget the Lord when they revel in plenty, but know the Lord very well when in want ... Do not associate with people who do not know how to obtain their food by sweat and labor, but, in disregard for law, plunder other people's property ... Do not associate with, or resemble such people as are impious in the extreme, and as good as comdemned to death ... do not be a pederast, or like such people ... do not be an adulterer or seducer, or like people of that stamp ... Associate with those who fear the Lord, with those who meditate on the precise sense of the words they have heard, with those who have the Lord's commandments on their lips and observe them, with those who realize that meditation is the labor of joy and therefore ruminate on the Word of the Lord. *Letter of Barnabas* 10[10]

[10]SC 172, 148-158

In contrast to the ancient lawgiver, Moses, the author makes no claim to teach with authority. Nevertheless, he feels it his duty to warn these recent converts against the dangers of worldly perversity, and of the attacks against their faith and morals that are and will be made through the impulse of the evil one, the devil. Finally he insists that "no man is an island" in the spiritual life. It is in the Christian assembly - "where two or three are gathered together in my name " - sharing grace-giving activities, and mutually discussing the Word of God, that the individual and the Christian community will grow up into the kingdom of God. The assurance that God in the final judgment will consider, not a person's status but his actions, similarly has a New Testament ring.

This chapter is an example, in the moral sphere, of the thesis enunciated by Barnabas that the ancient Jewish people mistook the Mosaic teaching, and that by applying the lawgiver's prohibitions of using certain animals for food literally, they wandered far from the truly spiritual meaning of the Old Testament. Actually, Barnabas is incorrect in his explanation, for the hygienic laws were meant to be taken literally. They were abolished by Christ when he established the New Testament in his church.

Barnabas follows a rather crude physiology of the mating habits of the hare and hyena to insist by way of contrast that human beings should cultivate a sanctifying purity in their moral life as becomes the people of God. Unnatural vices were widespread among the pagans and were frequently caricatured and deplored by moralists and satirists such as Juvenal and Martial. These same vices were not unknown among the Jews, and had been severely condemned by the prophets. To counter the temptations of such sins, the author proposes a positive engagement in the Christian community's spiritual life that should result in a joyful understanding and peaceful possession of the Word of the Lord.

See to it that the temple of God is built in splendor! How? Let me tell you. By receiving the forgiveness of sins and trusting in the Name, we were made new, being created all over again. That is why in our little house - in us - there really dwells God. How? By his word of faith; his calling us to the promised blessing, the wisdom of his ordinances, the precepts of his teaching, the fact that he personally prophesies in us and personally dwells in us, that he opens to us the door of the temple, that is, our mouth; that he grants us a renewal of spirit, that is what ushers us into the imperishable temple, us, I say, who had been enslaved to death! And in fact, when one is anxious to be saved, one pays no attention to the man, but to him who dwells and speaks in him, and it is a surprise to him that he has never either heard him utter such words or had a desire to hear them. This is a spiritual temple which is now being built for God. *Letter of Barnabas* 16[11]

In pursuit of this actualization of the Christian way of life, Barnabas emphasizes an elan or mystique that pervades the temple of God that is to be built by grace within the heart of the believer. The divine presence in the individual Christian is guaranteed by the re-creation of the soul in the name of Jesus in baptism. The description of this process includes the implementation of faith by an adherence to God's commands and precepts. His use of a man's faculties to proclaim God's actual presence in his prophecies is a powerful witness to the conviction behind the instructor's own faith. However, Pseudo-Barnabas insists that it is not the man, but the presence of God's Word in him, that produces salvation, and that enables the one anxious to be saved to become the living temple of God.

Let us now pass on to another kind of knowledge and instruction. There are Two Ways of instruction, as there are two powers, that of light and that of darkness. And there is a great difference between the Two Ways. The one is controlled by God's light-bearing angels; the other, by the angels of Satan. And as the latter is the ruler of the present era of lawlessness, so the former is Lord from eternity to eternity.

19. The Way of Life is as follows: whoever desires to make his way to the appointed place must work actively. The knowledge granted us to enable us to walk in this way embraces the following points. Love your maker; reverence your creator; glorify him who ransomed you from death; be single-minded and exuberant of spirit; do not associate with such as walk in the Way of Death.

Abhor everything not pleasing to God; detest every form of hypocrisy; do not by any means neglect the commandments of the Lord. Do not carry your head high, but be ever in a humble frame of mind; do not reach out for personal glory; do not plot evil against your neighbor; do not open your heart to presumption. Do not fornicate; do not commit adultery; do not practice pederasty; do not let the Word of God escape your lips in the presence of any that are impure ...

Love your neighbor more than yourself. Do not kill a fetus by abortion, or commit infanticide. Do not withdraw your hand from your son or your daughter; but from their youth teach them the fear of God ... Do not be on intimate terms with the powerful, but associate with holy and lowly folk. Accept as blessings the casualties that befall you, assured that nothing happens without God. Do not be double-minded or double-tongued, for a double tongue is a deadly snare. In reverence and fear be submissive to your masters as representatives to God ... Day and night remember the day of Judgment ... Are you proficient in speaking? Then go to comfort and

endeavor to save an afflicted soul. Do you work with
your hands? Then pay a ransom for your sins. *Letter of
Barnabas* 18-19[12]

In his enumeration of the sins to be avoided, the author
gives a catalog of the sexual vices that were common in all
the cities of the Roman Empire. Considerable knowledge of
these perversions has been gleaned from the works of the
dramatists and the satiric poetry of Horace, Martial and
Juvenal, all of whom wrote during this period. What is
obvious from the pagan Roman witness is that these practices were considered sins even by the pagans. Indulgence in
them, though taken for granted, was held up to ridicule as
demonstrating moral weakness. Among the Jews and Christians they were considered a double abomination as signify-
ing not only human frailty, but also a failure to use God's
protective graces. Yet they were dealt with frankly and
without excessive severity.

In this regard, the admonition of the father of the family
not to spare the rod or "not lay his hand on his children or
slaves lightly" has immediate significance. In well-directed
families, the mother had charge of the children, usually with
the aid of slaves as guardians (pedagogues) and nurses.
When the child reached maturity, the father's immediate
authority came into play. But before this, he still had an
obligation to correct and control his household. If he did so
properly, his children were brought up with due reverence
for their elders and "in the fear of the Lord."

There is no mention of either divorce or birth control
here, because evidently neither of these problems was immediately pertinent to the families being addressed. The early
Christians were supposed to love all their fellow men; hence,
in marriage, they strove to achieve great mutual respect and
love, imitating the love between Christ and his Church.
Among the devout, where marriages were arranged by the
heads of families, a gradual growth in conjugal love could be

taken for granted. Likewise, living in a society where many children were counted a great blessing, they were not tempted apparently to limit the size of their families.

> The Way of the Black One, on the other hand, is crooked and altogether accursed. It is the way to eternal death and punishment. In it is found everything that corrupts the souls of men: idolatry, rashness, the pomp of power ... Here belong persecutors of the good, haters of truth, lovers of falsehood, men ignorant of the reward for right living ... in a word, men steeped in sin. *Letter of Barnabas* 20-21[13]

> To sum up, when one has learned the just demands of the Lord, as contained in the scriptures, the proper thing is to make them the rule of one's life. Surely whoever complies with them will reap glory in the kingdom of God; whoever chooses the opposite course with all its works must perish. That is why there is a resurrection, why there is a retribution.

> I would exhort those who are in better circumstances, if they will accept my well-meant advice, you have in your community persons to whom you can do good; do not miss your opportunity! The day is at hand when all things will perish together with the Evil One. At hand is the Lord and his recompense! Again and again I exhort you: be your own good lawgivers; remain your own trusty advisers. Away with all hypocrisy! May God, who is Lord over the whole earth, grant you wisdom, understanding, insight, knowledge of his just demands, and patient endurance. Be learners in God's school, studying what the Lord requires of you; and then do it! Thus you will be approved on Judgment Day. *Barnabas* 21[14]

[13]SC 172, 210
[14]SC 172, 214-216

The string of vices that characterizes the Way of the Prince of Darkness was mentioned in the introductory essay. The additional warning about eternal damnation is certainly a reflection of the words of Christ in the Gospel.

In these final chapters there is considerable repetition, particularly in the admonition against hypocrisy that was so opposed to the highly valued singleness of heart or honesty of intention among the Jews. The eschatological reminder that the Lord was at hand, and the caution that they should be able to form their own consciences, are probably echoes of Pauline doctrine. Both these considerations are based on the cultivation of the virtues of wisdom, understanding, knowledge, and insight. The pragmatic injunction that once the Christian had studied the Lord's requirements, he should carry them out - Do it! - should appeal to the existentialist tendencies of the modern Christian. Actually, there appear to be many similarities between the world described by the Pseudo-Barnabas and contemporary culture. The reader should not deceive himself into thinking that, because this instruction is phrased in such apparently simple, even archaic sounding language, either the author or the original audience was simple-minded.

This doctrinal treatise ends with a discussion of Christian morality that flows out of the newness given to the convert through the name of Jesus and the remittance of sins. This spiritual rejuvenation is accomplished by the faith accepted with the wisdom of God's commands, and the precepts of his doctrine. Barnabas sets forth the particulars of his ethical teaching through the doctrine of the Two Ways. He is obviously under the influence of the Qumran community, for he speaks of the two powers, one of light and the other of darkness: the way of light is presided over by Lucifer, the angel of light; the way of darkness, by the Prince of Darkness. In many places, there is an almost *verbatim* convergence with the *Didache*, yet it would seem that both documents depend upon a common source, rather than upon one another. Characteristic of Barnabas is an insistence on the love of a personal God who cares for man, and urges him to simplicity of heart, humility, charity, and gentleness. All this is taught against the background of the resurrection, which will bring the great day of retribution.

The Letter of Clement of Rome to the Church in Corinth

This letter was written about A.D. 97, presumably by the bishop of Rome, though there is no indication of the authorship in the document. It is in the main a moral exhortation to peace and unity following an outbreak of rebellion on the part of the junior members of the Corinthian church. The letter ascribes this to "jealousy and envy" and describes the evils caused by these vices in the course of human history. He give examples from the Old Testament and from secular history, and he names Peter and Paul as victims of these vices.

The letter begins with a laudatory description of the peace and harmony that characterized the Church of Corinth where the "multitude of believers had but one heart and one soul." It describes their obedience to God's commands in mutual love, oblivious to the rank or station of individuals. The young were trained to temperance; wives, to the loving care of their household; citizens, to obey their rulers. They based their conduct on the imitation of Christ in his sufferings, and meditation on his blood.

> ... It is only a few rash and headstrong individuals who have inflamed your community to such a degree of madness that your venerable, widely renowned, and universally cherished name has been greatly defamed. Indeed was there ever a visitor in your midst who did not approve your excellent and steadfast faith? Or did not admire your discreet and thoughtful Christian piety? Or did not proclaim the magnificent character of your hospitality? Or did not congratulate you on your perfect and secure fund of knowledge? You certainly did everything without

an eye to rank or station in life, and regulated your conduct by God's commandments ... 2. Moreover, you were all in a humble frame of mind, in no way arrogant; practicing obedience rather than demanding it; happier in giving than in receiving. Being content with, and intent upon, the provision which Christ allowed you for your earthly pilgrimage, it was his words that you carefully locked up in your hearts, and his sufferings were ever before your eyes. Thus all were blessed with a profound and radiant peace of soul, and there was an insatiable longing to do good, as well as a rich outpouring of the Holy Spirit upon the whole community. Filled moreover with a desire for holiness, you stretched out your hands to almighty God, with ready good will and devout confidence, imploring him to show mercy in case you had inadvertently failed in any way ... *Letter of Clement* 1-2[15]

The introductory description of the full Christian life, for which the Church of Corinth was justly famous, was brought in as a literary device to obtain the good will of the readers to whom the writer intended later to deliver a strong reproof. At the same time it affords a realistic picture of life in an early Christian community, in a large metropolis of the Graeco-Roman world. The cultivation of virtuous practices from faith, through piety, to hospitality and knowledge or wisdom, follows the pattern of later New Testament teaching. The insistence on the practice of humility without concern for personal prerogatives has a local bearing: the letter is written to counteract rebellion. But it is also part of the basic mental attitude of the Christian imitating Christ's meekness. Finally, resignation to God's provident will, in conjunction with a conscious imitation of Christ's sufferings and passion, will be influential in forming Christian moral teaching in the following generations.

This ideal situation suddenly gave way to dissension and bickering.

[15]SC 167, 98-102

Brethren, jealousy and envy brought on fratricide on the part of Cain. Jealousy was the cause of our father Jacob's flight from his brother Esau ... Because of jealousy David not only incurred the envy of strangers, but was even persecuted by Saul, King of Israel ... *Letter of Clement* 4[16]

The insistence that jealousy and envy are the principal causes of great evil throughout human history is capped with the assertion that Peter and Paul, the two great apostolic athletes in the arena of life, were put to death as a result of these vices. The reference is wider than the ordinary meaning of these words. It introduces the notion of demonic influence brought to bear on evil men in the state and society, who want to destroy those who do God's will, and who manifest his goodness in the world.

The letter portrays the measures of Christian moral teaching and practice that should restore harmony in Christ. It insists on respect for "our traditions," and reminds the community of the authority in the Church that came from God to Christ, from Christ to the apostles, and from the apostles to those sent by them (42:1-5). Penance and conversion, as virtues to be found among pagans as well as Christians, are recommended as leading to peace and order.

Among the pagans, of course, the idea of conversion was common. It was on the lips of every wandering philosopher and preacher from the Stoics and Pythagoreans to the Cynics and Epicureans. The Stoics considered *metanoia* or conversion as a turning from immersion in worldly affairs to a life of contemplation in which one strove to meditate on the True, the Good, and the One. This last was a transcendent being, the source of all that exists. But their notion of God was involved in pantheism; they never achieved the idea of a truly spiritual being since they thought matter inseparable from spirit. The Epicureans, on the other hand, believed that what was natural was good; they likewise preached a conversion to what the French call *spirituel* - a

[16]SC 167, 106

reasonable use of the mind in all man's interests, intellectual as well as material. The author of this letter to the Corinthians is obviously a man of the world in this *spiritual* sense. So aware is he of the literary and cultural interests of the late first century that a monograph has been written to prove that he was a convert from Stoicism. It is all but certain, however, that he was a convert from Judiasm, well schooled in secular culture:

> We are writing this, beloved, not merely for your admonition, but also to serve as a reminder to ourselves; for we are in the same arena, and face the same conflict. Let us then give up those empty and futile aspirations, and turn to the glorious and venerable rule of our tradition. Let us attend to what is noble, what is pleasing, what is acceptable in the sight of our maker. Let us fix our gaze upon the blood of Christ, and understand how precious it is to the Father, because, poured out for our salvation, it brought to the whole world the grace of conversion. Let us pass in review all the generations and learn the lesson from generation to generation, that the master has given an opportunity for conversion to those who were willing to turn to him. Noe preached the need of conversion, and such as heeded him were saved. Jonas announced destruction to the Ninevites; they did penance for their sins and by their prayer propitiated God and gained salvation, although they were not of God's own people. *Letter of Clement* 7[17]

The author's attitude throughout is benign. While positive in his admonition and directives, he demonstrates a true humility, calling attention to the necessity of practicing what he himself preaches. The references to the arena - the Christian exposed to the wild beasts of temptation like a gladiator fighting for his life on exhibition in a Roman sport - is characteristic of similar *mise-en-scene* taken from daily life in Rome and Corinth, that enliven the descriptions

[17]SC 167, 110-112

throughout the letter. The letter insists on the continuity of God's providence, and it offers saints of the Old and New Testaments as models of faith, hospitality, and perseverance for contemporary Christians. Finally, the reference to the Ninevites as pagans capable of salvation indicates a consciousness of the Church's mission to all mankind.

> The spirit of humility and modesty, therefore ... has been helpful not only to us, but also ... to those who have received his words in fear and truth. And so, since we are allowed to profit by so many glorious examples, let us hasten on to the goal of peace handed down to us from the beginning. Let us fix our gaze upon the Father and creator of the whole world, and hold fast to his magnificent and superabundant gifts and the blessings of peace. Let us see him in spirit, and contemplate with the eyes of the soul, his forbearing disposition; let us consider how unimpassioned he is in dealing with all of his creation.

> 20. The heavens revolve by his arrangement, and are subject to him in peace ...

> 21. Take care, beloved, that his blessings, numerous as they are, do not turn to our condemnation in case we do not - through a life unworthy of him - do with perfect accord what is good and pleasing in his sight ... Rather than to God, let us give offense to foolish, unreasoning men; to men conceited, and arrogantly indulging in boastful speech. Let us reverence the Lord Jesus Christ, whose bood was sacrificed for us; respect our officials; honor the presbyters; subject the young to the discipline of the fear of God; train our wives in all that is good. Let the latter exhibit lovable and chaste manners, show forth a sincere and gentle disposition; by their silence let them manifest their courtesy of speech; without partiality let them perform their works of charity, and with a pure intention bestow them equally on all that fear God. Our

children must have their share of a Christian upbringing;
they must learn how effective with the Lord is a humble
frame of mind; what holy love can accomplish with God;
how honorable and excellent is the fear of him; and how it
brings salvation to all who in this fear lead holy lives, with
a conscience undefiled ...

To all these precepts of faith Christ gives stability; for he
himself through the Holy Spirit calls us to him ... The
all-merciful and beneficent Father has compassion on
such as fear him; willingly and with tender regard he
bestows his graces on such as approach him single-
mindedly. Therefore let us not be double-minded, and let
not our soul mistrust him, seeing his gifts are all-
surpassing and glorious ... *Letter of Clement* 19-23[18]

These reflections follow a series of examples of virtuous
conduct, and are built around the four virtues of humility,
modesty, peacefulness, and fear of the Lord. The spiritual
nature of God who can only be seen with the eyes of the soul
is in contrast to the idols of other religions; and the remark
regarding God's forbearance in dealing with man, has reference to the charge that the calamities of the Roman Empire
are due to divine displeasure with the Christians because
they do not worship the civic gods. There is no doubt that
popular feeling against Christians was based on this fact.
Clement's contention is that in this respect God appears
almost indifferent to man's doings; otherwise his punish-
ments would be infinitely greater in dealing with the human
race.

The description of the orderliness of the heavens as a
model for man's regulating his way of life reflects both the
later Jewish Psalms and Wisdom literature, as well as Stoic
doctrine about the cosmos. The argument is concluded with
the observation that if inanimate creation obeys God, then
men in their various capacities - citizens, laity, wives, and

[18]SC 167, 132-140

children - owe an immediate subjection to their superiors. But here the true motivation is supplied: reverence for the patience and sufferings of Christ whose blood was shed for us.

In the lengthy explanation of the duties of wives, little attention is paid to their social standing in the eyes of the Church. It is difficult for modern readers to appreciate fully the role played by women in ancient Roman and Hebrew society and, as a result, in the early Church. While the husband was head of the household and had almost the only legal rights, women controlled many phases of ancient life. They ran the household completely. Mainly by indirection; they influenced their husbands in public affairs. Occasionally, of course, ancient women appear in history as princesses or powerful concubines who actually govern, and make or break courtiers; nor were they without education or influence in religious matters. But since the state religion of the Romans and the Hebrews' service of God were matters of public cult, the man was in charge. This was believed to be dictated by divine ordinance.   Nevertheless, widows and older virgins played a considerable role in the spread of the Gospel - most of Paul's references to friends in his letters are to women! and in the development of the early Christian way of life.

It is obvious, too, that the type of fear Clement is inculcating in children is reverence rather than abject subjection, for it is combined with love. The type of family life described here is almost ideal, and its foundation is the grace afforded by the Holy Spirit in reward for faith. This faith includes the security of the resurrection which God, through the scriptures, holds before the Christian as his supreme goal. And God's veracity is used as an exemplar for man's avoidance of lying.

> Let us consider how the Master continually calls our attention to the future resurrection, the first fruits of which he has made the Lord Jesus Christ by raising him from the dead ...27. He who enjoined us not to lie, will

for that reason be himself all the less capable of lying; for nothing is impossible to God except being untrue to himself ... *Letter of Clement* 24[19]

Since, then, we are a holy portion, let us do nothing but what makes for holiness, shunning slander, foul and sinful embraces, drunkenness, revolutionary desires, and abominable passions, detestable adultery and abominable pride ... Let us associate with those on whom divine grace has been bestowed; let us with humble minds put on the livery of concord and self-restraint; keep ourselves free from all backbiting and slanderous talk; and let us seek justification by actions, and not just words ...

So we, too, who have been called by his will in Christ Jesus, are sanctified not through ourselves, or through our wisdom or understanding or piety, or any works we perform in holiness of heart, but in the faith through which almighty God has sanctified all men from the beginning of time ... What then are we to do, brethren? Shall we rest from doing good, and give up love? May the master never permit that this should happen, at least not to us; but let us be eager to perform every good work with assiduity and readiness ... 34. The good workman with assurance receives the bread of his labor; the slack and slothful cannot look his employer full in the face. It is our duty, therefore, to be prompt to do good; for on him depends everything ... *Letter of Clement* 30-33[20]

The realism of the third last paragraph must strike the reader as capable of immediate modern application; in these fundamental failings of human nature, the world does not change very much. In dealing with the so-called problem of justification, Clement settles the difficulty in a practical fashion. God's grace through the redemption has restored

[19]SC 167, 142-144
[20]SC 167, 148-154

us to supernatural life in faith. Good works are the normal consequence of this state, particularly for Christians who proclaim love of neighbor as one of Christ's primary commands.

> How blessed and marvelous are the gifts of God! Life with immortality; joyousness with observance of the law; truth with boldness; faith with confidence; continence with holiness! And all these blessings even now fall within our comprehension ... Let us, therefore, exert ourselves to be found in the number of those who patiently wait for him, so that we may participate in the promised fight. But how, beloved, can this be done? If our mind is faithfully fixed on God; if we seek out what is pleasing and acceptable to him; if we carry out what his irreprehensible will demands, and follow the way of truth, by ridding ourselves of every vice ...

> Let us then do a soldier's duty in downright earnest under the banner of his glorious commands. Let us observe those who are soldiering under our commanders, and see how punctually, how willingly, how submissively they execute the commands. Not all are perfects, or tribunes, or centurions, or lieutenants; but each in his own rank executes the orders of the emperor and commanders.

> Therefore let the whole of our body be maintained in Christ Jesus; and let each submit to his neighbor's rights in the measure determined by the special gift bestowed on him. Let the strong care for the weak, and the weak respect the strong; let the rich support the poor; and the poor render thanks to God for giving them the means of supplying their needs. Let the wise man show his wisdom not in words but in active help. The humble man must not testify for himself, but leave it to another to testify in his behalf. He who is continent must not boast, knowing that it is another who confers on him the ability to remain continent ...

> Since therefore, this is evident to all of us, that we have explored the depths of the divine knowledge, we are obliged to carry out in fullest detail what the master has commanded us to do at stated times . . .

> Each of us, brethren, must in his own place endeavor to please God with a good conscience; reverently taking care not to deviate from the established rule of service . . .

> The apostles preached to us the gospel received from Jesus Christ, and Jesus Christ was God's ambassador. Christ, in other words, comes with a message from God; and the apostles, with a message from Christ . . . *Letter of Clement* 35, 37-38, 40-42[21]

The controlled enthusiasm of these considerations concerning the magnificence of the Christian experience should serve as a reassurance that the writer and the community to whom this document is directed partook of the expansive seriousness that is the backbone of true Christian culture. The guarantee of immortality becomes the immediate springboard to holiness, and activates a joyful observance of the law. This implies the fearless courage that St. Paul terms *parrhesia*: an intrepid openness in announcing the word of God, and in doing God's will in the world. What keeps this a virtue and therefore avoids arrogance or *hubris* - the incontinent riding over others' feelings or rights - is the disciplined acceptance of divine truth. Clement likens this to the situation in the Roman army - an institution known to all his contemporaries. What makes it at once supremely human and yet oriented to spiritual achievement is the active part played by divine charity and human love in combination to "cover a multitude of sins," and "preserve perfect harmony." This paragraph (49) echoes St. Paul's magnificent hymn to charity (1 Cor. 13:4-24). It is the essence of Christian moral doctrine that St. Augustine will reiterate as "love, and do what you will."

[21]SC 167, 156-158; 160-164; 166-168

He who has love in Christ must observe the commandments of Christ. The binding power of the love of God! -who is able to set it forth? The radiance of his beauty! -who can voice it to satisfaction? ... Love unites us with God; love covers a multitude of sins; love endures everything; is long-suffering to the last. There is nothing vulgar, nothing conceited in love; love creates no schisms; love does not quarrel; love preserves perfect harmony. In love, all the elect of God reached perfection; apart from love nothing is pleasing to God. *Letter of Clement* 49[22]

The Letters of Ignatius of Antioch

Ignatius of Antioch was sent as a prisoner from his native Antioch in Syria to Rome, and put to death there sometime during the reign of the Emperor Trajan, probably between A.D. 108 and 117. During the journey across Asia Minor, he stopped at the churches of Laodocea, Smyrna, Philadelphia and Ephesus, and sent seven letters: six addressed to the Christian communities at Ephesus, Magnesia, Tralles, Rome, Philadelphia and Smyrna. There is a final letter to Bishop Polycarp of Smyrna. Ignatius designates himself as the *theophorus* or God-bearer; in the *Letter to the Romans*, he begs them not to intervene with the authorities to have him set free, since he desires "as God's wheat to be ground by the teeth of wild beasts into Christ's pure bread."

While the authenticity of these letters is still disputed among scholars, there is now fairly general agreement that they are of the work of Ignatius, and that the style is in keeping with the so-called Asiatic manner of writing, proper to a well-educated Syrian of the 2nd century. In subject matter and attitude, the letters indicate a breaking away from the Jewish-oriented Pauline approach to the Mosaic law that conflicted with the law of Christ, in favor of the preoccupations of the Hellenists.

[22]SC 167, 180

Ignatius presents an answer to the Greek consciousness of death and the futility of earthly existence. He insists that Christ's death and resurrection are mysteries whereby man's salvation has been accomplished. This salvation consists in man's introduction to a new life, *zoe*, a sharing of the divine existence that guarantees immortality. This he contrasts with *bios*, the life tied to the experiences of earthly existence. *Zoe* implied a participation in the life-giving spirit, and Ignatius insisted that this was brought about through a complete transformation of mentality by regeneration in Christ, God and man, through participation in the eucharistic sacrifice that was the antidote of mortality (Eph. 20:2), since it allowed man to partake of the flesh and blood of Christ.

Against this background and within the Church presided over by the bishop, who is the living image of the invisible God (Magn. 6:1), Ignatius portrays the ethical obligations of the Christian. He must follow Christ in all things, and through Christ imitate his heavenly Father. But what is explicitly characteristic of the Ignatian approach to the Christian way of life is his insistence on union in the love of God and the imitation of Christ that constitute the Christian community.

> A church deserving of felicitation, blessed as she is with greatness, through the fullness of God the Father; predestined, before time was, to be forever, through real suffering, united and chosen in her abiding and unchanging glory, by the will of the Father, and of Jesus Christ, our Lord.
>
> With joy in God I welcomed your community, which possessed its dearly beloved name because of a right disposition, enhanced by faith and love through Christ Jesus our Savior. Being imitators of God, once restored to new life in the blood of God, you have perfectly accomplished the task so natural to you. *Ephesians* 1[23]

[23]SC 10, 56

In his letter to the Ephesians, Ignatius addresses the people of God in the Church at Ephesus and bases his exhortations on the fullness of divine life that these Christians exhibit; he expresses his satisfaction with the fervor they have achieved through suffering for the love of God. He emphasizes the fact that the Church was conceived by God before the beginning of time, and traces its present glory to its attachment to Christ and to God in faith and love — two primary virtues that Ignatius will mention some forty times in the course of these short letters. He maintains that faith is the beginning, and love the completion of the Christian life in God.

In similar fashion, Ignatius writes to the Church at Philadelphia.

> . . . . This church I salute in the blood of Jesus Christ. She is the source of everlasting joy, especially since her members are at one with the bishop and his assistants, the presbyters and deacons, who have been appointed in accordance with the wish of Jesus Christ; and whom he has, by his own will, through the operation of his Holy Spirit, confirmed in loyalty. *Salutation*[24]

The Church is the community whose structure is supplied by the bishops, priests, and deacons in harmony, imitating God's oneness and holiness, and nourished with the blood of Christ. The source of everlasting joy, the Church is confirmed in its loyalty to God by the Holy Spirit; therefore, its members should live in harmony, meditating on the mind of God.

> . . . . Live in harmony with the mind of God. Surely, Jesus Christ is our inseparable life; for his part is the mind of the Father, just as the bishops, though appointed throughout the vast, wide earth, represent for their part the mind of Jesus Christ . . . How much more do I count you happy who are as closely knit to him (your bishop) as the Church is to Jesus Christ, and Jesus Christ is to God

[24]SC 10, 120

the Father. As a result, the symphony of unity is perfect. Let no one decieve himself: unless a man is within the sacred precincts, he has to go without the bread of God ... It follows then, he who absents himself from the common meeting, by that very fact shows pride and becomes a sectarian ...

7. Some people are, you know, accustomed with vicious guile to go about with the Name on their lips, while they indulge in practices at variance with it, that are an insult to God. These you must shun ... There is only one physician, both carnal and spiritual, born and unborn, God become man, true life in death; sprung both from Mary and from God; at first subject to suffering, then incapable of it — Jesus Christ Our Lord ...

The carnal cannot live a spiritual life, nor can the spiritual live a carnal life, any more than faith can act the part of infidelity, or infidelity the part of faith. But even the things you do in the flesh are spiritual, for you do all things in union with Jesus Christ. *Ephesians* 3-8[25]

While realistic almost to a fault, Ignatius still insists that man's basic desire for happiness is fulfilled in the Church through reception of the bread of God. However, this participation is reserved to those who accept Christ in the person of his Church with its teaching and commandments. Those who will not acknowledge the true faith, such as the Docetists (who maintained Christ had only an apparent body), should not call themselves Christians or use the name of Christ. Faith consists in the acceptance of Christ, true God and true man, as our only physician, whose sufferings in the flesh have not only restored man's immortality, but have sanctified the flesh itself. Hence, the true Christian acting in the flesh, is not destroying spiritual values.

[25]SC 10, 60-64

You consider yourselves stones of the Father's temple,
prepared for the edifice of God the Father, to be taken
aloft by the hoisting engine of Jesus Christ, that is the
cross; while the Holy Spirit serves you as a rope. Your
faith is your spiritual windlass; and your love, the road
that leads up to God ... *Ephesians* 9[26]

Again faith and love are considered the stones being built
into the temple of God within the believer; they are
emplaced and secured by the cross of Christ, and the action
of the Holy Spirit. The revelance of this comparison is
known from the fact that in the early 2nd century, great
building construction took place in Antioch. The author,
therefore, was familiar with the hoisting procedures used in
putting heavy building materials, such as great slabs of
stone, into place.

But pray unceasingly also for the rest of men, for they
offer grounds for hoping that they may be converted, and
win their way to God. Give them an opportunity, at least
by your conduct, of becoming your disciples. Meet their
angry outbursts with your own gentleness, their boastfulness with you humility, their revilings with your prayers,
their error with you constancy in the faith, their harsh-
ness with your meekness; and beware of trying to match
their example. Let us prove ourselves their brothers
through courtesy. Let us strive to follow the Lord's example and see who can suffer greater wrong; who more
deprivation, who more contempt. Thus no weed of the
devil will be found among you; but you will persevere in
perfect chastity and sobriety through Jesus Christ, in
body and soul. *Ephesians* 10[27]

The Christian must spread the gospel; but first he must
pray for all men, so that they may receive the great blessing

[26]SC 10, 64-66
[27]SC 10, 66

of the faith. The least the Christian can do is edify those outside the Church by the good example of his own way of life. This is, of course, a frequent admonition in the New Testament. It requires the practice of infinite forbearance through heroic charity in obedience to Christ's command to love one's enemies as described in St. Paul's magnificent hymn to charity (1 Cor. 13). Since Ignatius himself was a victim of anti-Christian persecution, his admonition to forgiveness of grave injuries inflicted by the enemies of Christ had double weight. But he goes further. Even common courtesy is not to be neglected, for it is a sign that a man truly considers his neighbor as his brother.

> Make an effort to meet more frequently to celebrate God's eucharist and to offer praise. For when you meet frequently in the same place, the forces of Satan are overthrown, and his baneful influence is neutralized by the unanimity of your faith.

> Peace is a precious thing; it puts an end to every war waged by heavenly or earthly enemies.

> 14. Nothing of this escapes you; only persevere to the end in your faith, and in your love for Jesus Christ. This is the beginning and the end of life: faith is the beginning, the end is love; and when the two blend perfectly with each other, there is God. Everything else that makes for right living is consequent upon these. No one who professes faith sins; no one who possesses love hates ...

> 3. So then, for the honor of him who has deigned to choose us, it is proper to obey without any hypocrisy. It is not really that a man deceive this particular bishop who is visible, but that he tries to overreach him who is invisible. When this happens, this reckoning is not with man, but with God who knows what is secret.

The proper thing is not merely to be styled Christ's, but also to be such ... *Ephesians* 13-14; *Magnesians* 3-4[28]

Ignatius urges the frequent gathering of the Christians to celebrate the eucharist and praise God, realizing, as does the Pseudo-Barnabas, the need for constant prayer and action to protect faith and fervor. This is the authentic doctrine of the mystical body of Christ present in the world through the continued repetition of this redeeming sacrifice, and the Christian's active participation in the mysteries of the Church's earthly life.

One who truly believes cannot knowingly offend God. He who truly loves Jesus Christ cannot hate anyone. Thus, the admonition not to try to deceive the bishop, since one cannot deceive God, is a direct conclusion; and the remark that one should not seek merely to be known as a Christian, but should actually belong totally to Christ, is a final conclusion from this premise.

> ....I exhort you to strive to do all things in harmony with God: the bishop is to preside in the place of God, while the presyters are to function as the council of the apostles, and the deacons who are most dear to me, are entrusted with the ministry of Jesus Christ ... Conform yourselves to God's ways, and respect one another, and let one regard his neighbor with the eyes of the flesh, but love one another at all times in Jesus Christ. *Magnesians* 6-7[29]

The reference to the eyes of the flesh is a Pauline consideration. Paul separates the spiritual-minded man, whose course is set in God and Christ, from the carnal-minded,

[28]SC 10, 68-70, 82
[29]SC 10, 82-84

whose desires and interests are directed solely to the things of this world. The admonition not to love in the flesh, then, does not exclude ordinary affection, on a sensual level. It does ban sinful desires or attachments. It is true love for God and for Christ that combines with spiritual and affectionate love for one's neighbor in Christ. It dictates the harmony in prayer and hope and charity that characterizes the Christian worship.

The danger that this admonition pinpoints is twofold. On the one hand, it is directed against every species of dualism that considers the flesh as evil since it is a material creation in contrast to spiritual goodness which can only be immaterial. This is heresy, of course, for it denies that God is the creator of the material universe and of man's body. Believers in such a doctrine required either perfect abstention from all bodily pleasures, particularly those connected with sex, or they permitted complete anarchy in sexual relations, only advising precautions against pregnancy. They reasoned that what was related to material things was evil, and did not count in the world of spiritual reality.

On the other hand, with St. Paul, the writer condemns the person whose whole interest is in earthly things, especially sexual pleasures, even though he would admit spiritual values in theory. Such a person is geared away from the true God and makes the things of this world his god.

In current psychological thinking there is a desire to return to the Pauline way of considering man - to get away from the dichotomy of soul and body, and to deal with the whole man, the psychosomatic (soul-body) individual. This is in keeping with early tradition of the Church that has always considered the body sacred, and insisted that in the resurrection man will possess soul and body, that he will be a whole man in eternity. Even the explanation of death as a separation of the body and soul, allowing the latter to exist in an incorporeal state, is being reconsidered today. The custom of referring to the soul alone - "save your soul!" -always had been understood to mean that with the soul went the body, even though too much emphasis was placed on sins committed with the body. Traditionally, however, sins of the spirit such as pride, avarice, and uncharitableness have always been considered more malicious than "the weakness of the flesh."

> Let us not, then, be insensible to his loving kindness. Certainly if he were to imitate our way of acting, we should be undone instantly. We must, therefore, prove ourselves his disciples, and learn to live like Christians ... Assuredly whoever is called by a name other than this, is not of God ...
>
> It is absurd to have Jesus Christ on the lips, and at the same time live like a Jew. No, Christianity did not believe in Judaism, but Judaism believed in Christianity, and in its bosom has assembled everyone professing faith in God. *Magnesians* 10[30]

In a sharp reminder of the instability of mere human love, Ignatius points out how truly hopeless man's situation would be if God were to treat us with the insensitivity and inconsistency with which one person so frequently treats another.

The practical admission of the original dependence of Christianity on Judaism is heartening, particularly in view of the polemical approach that Ignatius, along with most early Christian teachers, took toward the Jews. This hostility must be understood, however, as due to the immediate situation. Christianity had broken with Judaism; yet many of its adherents were converts from the synagogue, and a considerable attempt was being made to win them back to Judaism. On their side the Jews indulged in a strong polemic against the Christians as apostates from the true Jewish faith.

[30]SC 10, 88-90

... Take up the practice, then, of kind forbearance and renew yourselves in faith, which is the flesh of the Lord; and in love which is the blood of Jesus Christ. Let none of you bear a grudge against his neighbor. Give no pretext to the pagans, so that, despite a few foolish persons, God's own people may not be reviled ...

4. ... Take care, then, to partake of the eucharist; for one is the flesh of our Lord Jesus Christ; and one the cup to unite us with his blood; and one altar, just as there is one bishop assisted by the presbyter and the deacons, my fellow servants ...

8. ... Where there is division and passion, there is no place for God. Now the Lord forgives all if they change their mind, and by this change of mind, return to union with God and the council of the bishop. I trust in the grace of Jesus Christ, who will free you from all enslavement. *Trallians* 8; *Philadelphians* 4,8[31]

Ignatius admits to the difficulty of practicing the forbearance in regard to the Jews that should characterize the true Christian, and perhaps this is why he refers to himself as not yet a true disciple of Christ. However, there is also the possibility that he feels that only in death as a martyr will he be completing discipleship in full imitation of Christ. On the other hand, he insists that true love of neighbor is generated by the flesh and blood of Christ in which the Christian participates. So fortified, he must not give scandal to the pagans by demonstrating a hostile or disturbing spirit in dealing with opponents, be they Jews or pagan persecutors.

In his reference to bishops, presbyters or priests, and deacons in association in the eucharist, Ignatius witnesses to the hierarchical organization of the Church. He makes it clear that the power of orders given by Christ to the apostles, and handed on by them to their successors, is a neces-

[31]SC 10, 100; 122; 126

sary factor in celebrating the body and blood of Christ. Elsewhere he speaks of the bishop's authority in the Church. In his Letter to Polycarp, Ignatius advises:

> ... I exhort you, clothed as you are with the garment of grace, to speed on your course, and exhort all others to attend to their salvation. Do justice to your office with the utmost solicitude, both physical and spiritual. Be concerned about unity, the greatest blessing. Bear with all just as the Lord does with you ...

> ... Stand firm like an anvil under the hammer. It is like a great athlete to take punishment and yet win the fight. For God's sake above all, we must endure everything, so that God, in turn, may endure us. Increase your zeal. Read the signs of the times. Look for him who is above all time - the timeless, the invisible, who for our sake became visible; the one incapable of suffering, who became subject to suffering on our account ...

> Widows must not be neglected. After the Lord, you (the bishop) must be their guardians. Nothing must be done without your approval; nor must you do anything without God's approval, as indeed you do not. Be calm. Let meetings be held as frequently as possible. Seek out all by name. Do not treat slaves, male or female, with a haughty air; but neither must they give themselves airs. On the contrary, for the glory of God, they should render all the better service so as to obtain a better freedom from God. They should not pine for release at the expense of the community; otherwise they turn out to be slaves of unruly appetites ...

> Tell my sisters to love the Lord, and to be content with their husbands in body and soul. In like manner, exhort my brethren in the name of Jesus Christ to love their wives as the Lord loves the Church. If anyone is able to remain continent to the honor of the flesh of the Lord, let

> him persistently avoid boasting. The moment he boasts,
> he is lost ... *Letter to Polycarp* 1-5[32]

In his letter to Polycarp, finally, Ignatius points out the proper manner in which a true bishop is to conduct himself. There is the same emphasis on care for every member of the Church, and the admonitions to virtuous conduct of parents, masters and slaves, that characterize the other 2nd century Christian documents. His familiarity with the Pauline teaching on marriage, however, is unique among these early Christian teachers. It is an approach that our age finds most congenial as well as necessary to the contemporary problems of conjugal life. His praise of continence with his caution against pride or boastfulness echoed in the admonitions of the fathers down through Jerome, Ambrose, and Chrysostom to the end of the patristic age, more particularly when the practice of continence and virginity became a widespread institution in the Church.

The Ignatian moral teaching, it is obvious, cannot be separated from its roots in faith and love upon which are supported the Christian's imitation of Christ and God in his goodness and holiness.

[32]SC 10, 146-150

Chapter Two

The Greek Apologists

Letter to Diognetus

Among the early Christian catechetical documents is the so-called *Letter to Diognetus*, written in the form of a literary apology. The author is unknown. He addressed the work to a certain official, apparently of high rank, called Diognetus, who directed three questions regarding Christianity to the apologist. It is possible that this is a fictitious literary device, but the form and style of the letter make it a literary masterpiece as well as an excellent witness to the stature assumed by the Christian message, during the middle of the 2nd century.

The apologist answers three inquiries: What sort of religion is Christianity that it causes its adherents to spurn both the pagan gods and the superstition of the Jews? What is the secret of the affectionate love of Christians for one another? And, if Christianity is true, why did God hesitate so long in the course of human history before making it known to the whole of mankind?

In answering these questions, the author describes and rejects the pagan and Jewish way of life (ch. 1-4), defending the sanctity of the Christian ethic which he then explains at length. He closes with a consideration of the "mysteries of God the Father" in his eternal being (ch. 11 and 12). The authenticity of these last two chapters has been challenged, but, despite a definite break in style and continuity after chapter 10, they seem to be part of the original work.

The author describes the Christian way of life, after having denounced the diabolic iniquities of paganism, and refuted the charge of perversity and atheism brought against the Christians. He rejects the idea that Christians are a people apart, or a special race, as were the Jews within the Roman Empire, and insists that they belong to the Empire, even though they carry a double citizenship. It is a fact that Christians were referred to as pilgrims and passers-by on the earth (1 Peter 2:11), being citizens with the saints and members of God's household (Eph. 2:19), having citizenship in heaven (Phil. 3:20). Nevertheless, St. Paul also reminded them that since all authority is from God, they were to obey worldly rulers and respect and pray for kings and governors (Rom. 13:1-7; I Tim. 2:2). In fact, in the *Letter to Titus*, the Christians' loyalty to God is a further guarantee of the responsible way they perform their duties as citizens (Titus 3:1); continuing the tradition of the primitive Christian communities, they lead chaste family lives, but care for the poor. They share their possessions, but not their wives; and they pay their taxes and imposts, being worthy of admiration in keeping the laws.

> Christians are not distinguised from the rest of mankind by either country, speech, or customs. The fact is, they nowhere settle in cities of their own; they use no special language; they cultivate no eccentric mode of life. Certainly this creed of theirs is no discovery due to some fancy, or speculation of inquistive men; nor do they, as some do, champion a doctrine of human origin. Yet they dwell in both Greek and non-Greek cities, as each one's lot was cast. And they conform to the customs of the

country in dress, food, and mode of life generally. The whole tenor of their way of living stamps it as worthy of admiration, and as admittedly extraordinary. They reside in their respective countries, but only as pilgrims. They take part in everything as citizens, and put up with everything as foreigners. Every foreign land is their home, and every home, a foreign land. They marry like all others, and beget children; but they do not expose their offspring. Their board they share with all, but not thier bed. They find themselves in the flesh, but do not live according to the flesh. They spend their days on earth, but hold citizenship in heaven. They obey the established laws, but in their private lives they rise above all laws.

They love all men, but are persecuted by all. They are unknown, yet are condemned; they are put to death, but it is life that they receive. They are poor, and enrich many; destitute of everything, they abound in all things. They are dishonored, and in their dishonor, they find their glory. They are calumniated; and are vindicated. They are reviled, and they bless; they are insulted, and render honor. Doing good, they are penalized as evil-doers; when penalized, they rejoice because the are quickened into life. The Jews make war on them as foreigners; the Greeks persecute them; and those who hate them are at a loss to explain their hatred. *Letter to Diognetus,* 5[1]

The author's purpose is to demonstrate not only that Christians are not guilty of the crimes of infanticide, incest, and misanthropy of which they have been accused, but that they literally follow the command of Christ to love their neighbor, and out of the love of God, do good to them who hate and persecute them. Thus, the Christian life was based upon an interior conviction and a spiritual experience that were beyond the compass of the non-believer.

In asserting that the Christian tolerates all things, the author is referring to the restrictions put upon Christians by

[1]SC 33, 62-64

the persecutions, and their refusal to participate in public pagan religious sacrifices which offended their convictions. He then turns the argument to claim that, unlike their callous neighbors, they do not destroy unwanted children by abandoning them in the streets or on rubbish piles. They share their goods and food with members of their community, but are not guilty of immoral conduct with each others' wives. Continuing in the Pauline tradition, he maintains that they obey all the imperial laws, idolatry alone excepted.

> 6. In a word, what the soul is in the body, the Christians are in the world. The soul is spread through all the members of the body and Christians are spread throughout the cities of the world. *Letter to Diognetus*, 6[2]

> Immortal, the soul is lodged in a mortal element; so, too, Christians, though residing as strangers among corruptible things, look forward to the incorruptibility that awaits them in heaven. The soul, when stinting itself in food and drink, fares the better for it; in doing so Christians, when penalized, show a daily increase in numbers on that account. Such is the important post to which God has assigned them; and they are not at liberty to desert it. And no wonder. 7. It was not an earthly invention, as I have said, that was committed to their keeping. It was not a product of a mortal brain that they consider worth safeguarding so anxiously; nor have they been entrusted with the dispensing of merely human mysteries. Quite to the contrary! It was really the Lord of all, the creator of all, the invisible God himself, who, of his own free will, from heaven, lodged among men the truth and the holy, incomprehensible word, and firmly established it in their hearts ... *Letter to Diognetus*, 6-7[3]

[2]SC 33, 64
[3]SC 33, 66-68

In juxtaposing the incomparable mystery of the Christian message with the everyday actions of the individual who abstains not merely from food and drink, but from the corruptible things of the world, the author is purposely calling attention to the moral rectitude of the Christian way of life. By indirection, he contrasts it with Stoic philosophy that also stressed abstinence and a disregard for the pleasures of earthly things. Behind the Stoic philosophy, however, is an explanation of the universe by a sort of world soul that expanded and contracted, and thus caused what appeared to be the creation of material things, including man.

This philosophy the Christian considered nugatory in comparison with the sublime mystery of God as the Father and creator and of his Son as man's savior and redeemer. In safeguarding these mysteries, the Christian was not to hide them in esoteric language and exotic religious ceremonies, nor was he merely to contemplate them as the final end of his being. Rather he was to exemplify them in his daily conduct, thereby sanctifying himself by faithfulness in great and small deeds, and spreading the good word to all his fellow men.

The supervision of this adherence to the Christian mysteries of salvation early formed a tradition in the Church. Its main headquarters were located by St. Peter's in Rome, evidently in keeping with God's providence; and the Roman bishops from the beginning, according to the testimony of Irenaeus of Lyons (circa A.D. 190), were the custodians of traditional doctrine. As the sign of unity and the center of orthodoxy in the early Church, the bishops of Rome were appealed to by the other bishops, and their positions gradually became more eminent. For the most part, Rome's decisions were benevolent and middle-of-the-road when it came to witnessing and interpreting the principal Christian doctrines. Thus, in the 3rd century, Rome decided against the rebaptism of heretics; in the early 5th century, it took a generous position in the quarrel over the nature of grace insisting that, while it was the essential factor in holiness, it was also a great mystery.

> While he had already planned everything in his own
> counsels in union with the Son, he yet permitted us, all
> through the intervening time to be carried away, just as
> we chose, by unruly passions - the victims of unbridled
> desires. Not that he took delight at all in our transgres-
> sions. No, he merely exercised patience. Nor did he
> approve of that former period of wickedness; but on the
> contrary, was all the time shaping the present era of
> holiness. It was his intention that we, after our own
> conduct in the past had proved us unworthy of life,
> should now be rendered worthy by the goodness of God;
> and that, after we had demonstrated our inability, as far
> as in us lay, to enter the kingdom of God, we should be
> enabled to do so by the power of God. *Letter of Diogne-*
> *tus* 9[4]

The explanation of God's patience in respecting man's
free will, and his forbearance while man continues in sin is
an insistence upon reasonableness in the Christian attitude,
and a strong reminder of the part grace plays in conversion
and salvation. Thus, the accusation that Christianity came
late in the day of human history is turned aside by a reasonable explanation, pointing to the need of man's preparation
to accept it by means of a divinely guided education.

Justin Martyr (100-165)

Justin Martyr was a pagan born in Palestine who became
a Christian, and the most important of the Greek apologists
of the early Church. He described his journey from Stoicism
through the philosophies of the Peripatetics. Pythagoreans
and Platonists to Christianity in the course of his two *Apol-*
ogies and the *Dialogue with Trypho*, the Jew. These are the
only works of his that have been preserved. As a Christian, he
continued to wear the toga of a philosopher and traveled

[4]SC 33, 72

about as an itinerant preacher. He founded a school of Christian philosophy in Rome during the reign of Pius Antoninus (A.D. 138-161). He was put to death with a group of companions. The Acts of his martyrdom are an authentic record based upon the official court interrogation.

In the *First Apology*, Justin censures the attitude of the Roman authorities toward the Christians, since they believed false accusations and condemned a man merely for bearing the name Christian without proof of crimes. He contends that Christians are not atheists, because their eschatological beliefs, and the dread of eternal punishment, preserve them from wrongdoing, and, in fact, make them conscientious supporters of the Roman government. In the *Second Apology*, he defends the reputation of three Christians beheaded in Rome because they confessed their faith. He claims that the persecutions are instigated by the devils, and advises the Emperor of the superiority of the Christian way of life over the pagan superstitions. In the *Dialogue with Trypho*, he examines the claims of Christianity to be the religion foretold by the prophets, and gives a detailed development of his own conversion.

In his *First Apology,* Justin warns the pagans against the subtle wiles of Satan and summarizes the Christian moral code.

> 14. We advise you, [O pagans,] to beware lest the demons who were formerly served by us, should now deceive you and keep you from reading and understanding the things we have to say ... Now that we obey the Logos [or Word of God] we have deserted them, and follow the one true, almighty God through his Son. Once we rejoiced in impurities, now we embrace only continence; while we used magic arts in the past; now we are consecrated to the good and omnipotent God; where once we loved money and possessions above all else, now we turn over the few things we possess in common and bestow them on the most needy ... And lest we be thought to deceive you, we

believe it best to cite for you a few of the precepts of Christ himself ... his words are brief and circumspect, for he was not a sophist, but his word was the power of God.

15. Of chastity he said: Who looks after a woman with lust, has already committed adultery with her in his heart before God ... (Mt. 5:28).

Whoever enters a second marriage after divorce, according to human laws, are considered sinners before our judge, as well as those who gaze after a woman with cupidity. For not only he who actually commits adultery is rejected by him; but even he who desires to commit fornication. For not only our deeds, but our thoughts are known to God.

And there are many men and women of 60 and 70 years of age who have been disciples of Christ from their youth, and have remained uncorrupted; and I profess that I can show you such among every land and people. And we can remember a great, innumerable multitude who have been converted from an intemperate life, and learned these things. For Christ called not only the just and the chaste, but also the impious, and intemperate, and the unjust.

For his Heavenly Father desired the penitence of a sinner rather than his punishment ...

16. And he said that we were to be patient in evils, prepared to serve all, and not given to wrath ... He did not want us to be trouble-makers, or to imitate evil-doers; and he exhorted us to forbear with patience and meekness before indecency and the cupidity of the wanton. And indeed we can show these things concerning many who were among you: they have been changed from being violent and tyrannical; they were brought over either by seeing the constancy of the life of their neighbors, or by

recognizing the unheard-of patience in the life of our defrauded communities; or by experiencing this in those Christians with whom they did business. He (Christ) commanded us never to swear, and always to tell the truth ... And when someone approached him and said: "Good Master!" he replied: "No one is good but God alone, who has made all things." And those not living thus as he taught, should not be considered Christians; nor should those who profess the doctrines of Christ only with their tongue; for he said that not they who confess him, but they who do his works will be saved ... We would even desire that they who say they are Christians, but do not live in accordance with his doctrine, should be punished by you.

17. Before all things else we try to pay tribute and taxes to those who have been commissioned by you everywhere, just as we were taught by him. For in his day, certain ones approached him and asked whether it was proper to pay the tax to Caesar. And he answered: "Tell me, whose image is on the coin?" And they answered, "Caesar's." And he said to them: "Render therefore to Caesar the things that are Caesar's, and what is God's to God"(Luke 12:48).

Hence we adore one only God, and we happily serve you in all things else, acknowledging that you are the kings and princes over men, and praying that we may find you of sound judgment in your regal power. But if you neglect us though we pray for you, and display everything we have openly in the light, we will not consider it a loss, since we believe and are persuaded that each one according to his deserts will be punished in eternal fire; and that each one will have to render an account of the talents he has received. For Christ has declared: to whom God has given more, of him more will be required. *First Apology*, 14-17[5]

---

[5] *Florilegium Patristicum*, 2. 28-38, ed. Rauschen

Justin's remark that the pagans should take care was meant as a more or less ironic, though amusing, observation. He admits that as pagans, he and many converted Christians served the demons, as do the pagans still. Therefore, he warns his former co-religionists that, with so many people abandoning the demons, the latter will have more strength and power to attack those remaining in paganism to keep them from truly understanding the Christian message. His confession of former sins is, of course, a strong indictment of the pagans still involved in these practices.

What is so interesting about this part of the Apologia is the witness it gives to the effect of Christ's "speaking with authority," in short, concise, and clear moral admonitions. It was once thought that in the early Church, the Christians hid their doctrines from the pagans, following the so-called "rule of the secret" - *disciplina arcani*. Justin openly quotes both the moral teaching and the rule of faith. Hence, this secrecy was not observed until much later, when it was used to give the religion a more solemn aspect. The early Christians were proud to announce their beliefs and the benefits they brought individuals and the Empire. Justin's boast that many men and women of 60 and 70 years of age had kept the Christian faith from their youth was a powerful claim to publish before his contemporaries. It strikes us also as a very heartening fact. It was as hard to be a thorough Christian then as it is now. The reference to God's omniscience, as in all these early churchmen, comes from the Old Testament, and is part of the insistent claim that God is not only actively interested in man's affairs, but actually loves all human beings. This assertion was necessary to counter frequent tendencies to despair at the cold cruelty of the world with its calamities, and its harsh human laws and relationships.

In describing the Christians's attitude toward the state, Justin does not hesitate to acknowledge the legitimacy of taxes and imposts, and to claim that Christ taught the moral obligation to be just and honest in dealing with rulers and their demands.

On the other hand, he tells the rulers that while they occupy their positions because of special talents they have demonstrated, God is going to demand an even greater account of their doings.

> I will also tell you the manner in which we dedicate ourselves to God, when we have been made new through Christ; lest, if we omit this, we seem to be unfair in the explanation we are making.

> As many as are persuaded and believe that what we teach and say is true, and undertake to be able to live accordingly, are instructed to pray, and to entreat God with fasting for the remission of their sins that are past. And we pray and fast with them. Then they are brought by us where there is water, and are regenerated in the same manner in which we ourselves were regenerated. For in the name of God the Father and Lord of the universe; and of our savior Jesus Christ, and of the Holy Spirit, there they receive the washing with water ... And for this, we have learned from the apostles the reason. At our first birth, we were born without our knowledge and our choice, by our parents' coming together. We were brought up in bad habits and wicked training. Now in order that we may not remain the children of necessity and of ignorance, but may become the children of choice and knowledge, we may obtain in the water, the remission of sins formerly committed. Hence there is pronounced over him who chooses to be born again, and has repented of his sins, the name of God the Father, and Lord of the universe. He who leads to the washing the person that is to be washed calls him by this Name alone. And this washing is called illumination, because they who learn these things are enlightened spiritually.[6]

> 67. And on the day that is called Sunday, all who live in the cities or in the country, gather together in one place; and the memoirs of the apostles and the writings of the prophets are read as long as time permits. Then the reader

[6]FIP 2, 98-100

concludes, and the president verbally instructs and exhorts us to the imitation of these excellent things. Then we all rise together and offer up our prayers. And, as I said before, when we have ended our prayer, bread is brought and wine and water; and the president in like manner offers up prayers and thanksgiving according to his ability, and the people give their assent by saying "Amen."

And there is a distribution and partaking by everyone of the eucharist. And to those who are absent a portion is brought by the deacons. Those who are well-to-do and willing, give as they choose; each as himself purposes. The collection is then deposited with the president who supports widows, orphans, those who are in want owing to sickness or any other cause; those who are in prison, and strangers who are on a journey. In a word, he takes care of all who are in need. But Sunday is the day on which we hold our common assembly, because it is the first day on which God, when he changed darkness and matter, made the world. And Jesus Christ our savior on the same day, rose from and dead... *First Apology* 67[7]

Beginning with Chapter 61 of the Apology, Justin describes the baptismal and eucharistic ceremonies of the Church, again showing how closely aligned was Christian conduct with the mysteries of Christ's redemption and Christian belief in God's constant care for each human being.

Justin testifies to the fact that in his day Christian baptism was administered in running streams or rivers. His comment on the freedom of choice with which the convert decides to be reborn, in contrast to his fate in being born without recourse into a family, is somewhat ingenious. But it serves the purpose and stresses the freedom that leads to God's action in granting divine wisdom and grace in an illumina-

[7] *Flor. Pat.* 2. 108-110

tion of the soul. This conviction is necessary as a driving force in keeping the commandments, a driving force based on the objective fact of true faith. The description of the Sunday liturgy is both precious and precise and brings the reader back almost 17 centuries to find that the basic ceremonies of the eucharistic celebration have remained the same in the Church.

This whole chapter is a powerful witness to the strength of Christian ideas; celebrating Sunday as commemorating the tremendous fact of creation, as well as of the resurrection; putting that celebration in the spiritual context of participation in Christ's intimate life through receiving his body and blood; and finally, actively loving one's neighbor by providing for the poor, the sick, the downcast, and abandoned. Early Christianity was a powerful religion.

Tatian the Syrian

A Syrian by birth and a pagan, Tatian became a convert to Christianity in Rome where he had attended the school of Christian philosophy organized by Justin Martyr. In his *Discourse to the Greeks*, he describes his experience with various philosophies and false religions before becoming a Christian. When first he read the Scriptures, he was repelled by their unpolished language and anthropomorphic atmosphere, as St. Augustine would be two centuries later. However, on further investigation, he found their doctrine excellent. Through divine grace afforded him in the pursuit of the Word of God, he became a defender of the Christian faith. Unlike Justin, he rejected the pagan philosophies outright; his rigorism evidently increased with age, and after his return to the Orient (circa A.D. 172), he became a founder of the sect called the Encratites or Abstinents. It professed a Gnostic spirituality, rejected matrimony, and the use of meat and wine, going so far as to substitute water for wine in the eucharist. Its devotees were called *Aquarii*, or water-drinkers. Tatian published a *Diatesseron* or harmonization of the four gospels which has been preserved; his other writings, evidently prolific, have been lost.

The importance of Tatian as a witness to the development of Christian moral thought lay in his approach to the inner workings of the soul engaged in the struggle for salvation. He speaks of two spirits within man, the *psyche* and a higher presence based on the biblical *ruah* (spirit or breath of life). It is a participation in the divine in which man reflects the image and likeness of God (Disc. 12). The disobedience of man through Adam had a cosmic effect, including his expulsion from paradise, and in some way, his subjection in the *psyche* or soul to the influence of evil spirits. They taught him to worship false gods and idols. Salvation is possible through God's goodness and grace; it consists in the destruction of false allurements through man's search for divine truth, and the restoration of the divine spirit (*ruah*) within man.

> The spirits that are produced from matter, and who are far from right conduct are worshipped by you, O Greeks ... And the Lord of all has suffered them to conduct themselves freely until the world ends and is dissolved. The judge will then appear; and all those men who, though assailed by the demons, strove after knowledge of the perfect God, will obtain a more perfect testimony on the day of the judgment as a result of their conflicts. 13. The soul is not itself immortal ... Yet it is possible for it not to die ... If it knows not the truth, it dies with the body and will be dissolved, and will rise again in the final end of the world with the body to receive death by punishment forever. If, however, it aquires the knowledge of God, it will not die, although for a time it will be dissolved ...
>
> Now, in the beginning the spirit was a constant companion of the soul, but the spirit forsook it because it was not willing to follow. Yet, retaining, as it were, a spark of its power, though unable to discern what was perfect, it fashioned for itself many gods, in seeking God ... The

spirit of God is not with everyone; but takes up residence with those who live justly, and combines with the soul intimately, teaching it hidden things by prophecies that are to be told to other souls. *Discourse* 12-13[8]

You, O Greeks, are accustomed to obey the demons as if they were powerful. For as the thief often overcomes his equal by daring, so the demons have deceived souls among you by great wickedness, playing on your ignorance and false appearances. *Discourse, 14*[9]

Man is not, as the prating philosophers claim, merely a rational animal capable of understanding and knowledge; but man is the image and likeness of God ... not, of course, when he behaves like the animals; but when he acts like one who advances beyond humanity toward God himself. *Discourse* 15[10]

The Greeks, whom Tatian is addressing, are the educated people of his day; more properly, perhaps, they should be called the Hellenes. Greek was the language of the Roman Empire, hence of the Church; the education was that of the Hellenistic *paideia* or pedagogy. As a Syrian, Tatian could have been indicating his different national origin and claiming superiority for the "barbarian" Christian creed over the accepted high standard of Hellenism. It is more likely, however, that he is using a formula common to the *Discourse*.

Almost all religions and philosophies acknowledged the existence of demons and their ability to influence men and nations. Even today it can be said that our time has its demons, although they are not conceived in the crude anthropomorphic terms of earlier ages. Many phenomena, formerly ascribed to demons, are now seen as the result of

[8]OECT, ed. Whittaker, 25
[9]OECT, 29
[10]OECT, 30.

neurotic forces and social frenzies that give rise to individual and national psychoses. Tatian explains the Christian view of man's creation and the freedom he obviously enjoyed despite the internal pressures that are responsible for his sinfulness. He is combating a dualistic, gnostic explanation that believed in a principle of evil and, therefore, in two basically opposed gods responsible for creation. One is the god of evil who brought material things into existence; the other, the god of goodness who presides over the spiritual world.

The more perfect testimony on the last day is no doubt Christ's promise: "He who confesses me before men, him I will confess before my Heavenly Father" (Mt. 10:32). Tatian's eschatological doctrine concerning man's end, and the final destruction of the world is strictly biblical. His idea concerning the nature of the soul with its *psyche* or intelligence and a still higher faculty capable of entertaining the divine spirit are in keeping with the Old Testament concept of the *shekinah* or God's presence, obtained through the contemplation of divine wisdom in a higher part of the soul. There is a relation with the Greek notion of the *nous* or higher reasoning faculty, but the main inspiration is scriptural.

The analogy with a thief overcoming his victim by cleverness and daring is interesting. Tatian, thus, applies a thoroughly rational explanation of the demons' power and says, in effect, that God's grace enables man with courage to outmaneuver the tempter. This ability comes with prayer and the vigilant search for holiness.

In general, Tatian is opposed to an intellectual approach to Christian teaching, and particularly to a rationalization of the Church's moral doctrine. He maintains that only among simple-minded barbarians was a pure attitude toward natural law preserved. And he attacked the decadence of the hellenistic and Roman civilizations with withering venom. In the end, of course, he trailed off into heresy, as did Tertullian, another over-vigorous critic of the Church's attempt to fit its moral teaching to the needs of the time. While Christ preached simply and used figures and parables mainly to present his doctrine to his unlearned audiences, there is great profundity in his doctrines of the Trinity and the redemption, and in his interpretation of the commandments and the demands of the Sermon on the Mount. In each age, his words need interpretation, as St. Augustine clearly saw, and that interpretation requires a knowledge of worldly science, literature, and philosophy.

Only sheer intellectual laziness or snobbism would suggest that one can understand the gospel without broad knowledge, however simple it seems at first reading. Experiments in a fundamentalist interpretation of the scriptures by various sects have eventually bogged down in a literal interpretation that simply does not represent the authentic Christian message. The letters of St. Paul, in which the author of Peter's epistle says there are "many things hard of understanding," indicate the care needed to interpret the gospels. And there is nothing simplistic or anti-intellectual about Paul, even when he condemns worldly philosophies. He is condemning intricate and inept attempts to explain mysteries, but his own moral doctrine is well-argued and formulated with intellectual vigor. It requires fortitude and intelligence of the reader as well as the commentator. Tatian appreciated this and dropped Paul from among his favorite authors when he put together his *Diatesseron*.

Irenaeus of Lyons

The development of the Church's moral doctrine during the primitive period is brought together in a logically coherent consideration of man as a moral being by Irenaeus, bishop of Lyons. A disciple of Polycarp of Smyrna, Irenaeus left Asia Minor and settled in Gaul, where in 177 or 178 he was a priest, and was sent to Rome to discuss with Pope Eleutherius the question of Montanism. On his return north, he was elected bishop of Lyons in place of Photinus. He wrote to Pope Victor suggesting forbearance in the pope's desire to excommunicate the Asiatic Christians who followed Jewish custom in celebrating the date of Easter. He seems to have been martyred toward the year 200.

His primary work is the *Detection and Overthrow of the Pretended but False Gnosis*, known generally as the *Adversus Haereses* or *Against Heresies*. His *Demonstration of the Apostolic Preaching* has also been preserved for posterity. His contributions to the development of the Church's theology is crucial, particularly in the development of its doctrine of Trinity, Christology, Mariology, and its concepts regarding the nature of the Church or ecclesiology, the Roman primacy, the eucharist, eschatology, and the canon of Scriptures.

Irenaeus begins his theological considerations with a refutation of the pessimistic evaluation of evil as a positive reality that was the doctrine of the Gnostics. This dualistic movement, that had infected both pagan and Jewish thought, had also become a heretical Christian sect. It idolized the so-called *pneumatic* or spiritual man, and despised the sensual or *sarkic* man. In his refutation, Irenaeus retains the Semitic division of man into flesh, soul, and spirit that is proper to Pauline thinking. He argues against the Gnostics on the essential unity of the human composite, again within a Semitic context. In so doing, he elaborates a Christian anthropology that has its roots in the Pauline conception of the incarnation of Christ.

The moral teaching of Irenaeus flows from his concept of man's redemption. Man is redeemed in Christ who became the new Adam. As a man betrayed the human race, so a man had to redeem mankind. The act of salvation was acceptable to God because Christ was also true God. Two soteriologies were to be developed from this concept. Tertullian and the Western theologians would stress the repayment of the debt to God; Athanasius and the Orientals, man's divinization in Christ who joined the divine nature to a human body and soul.

> Man has received the knowledge of good and evil. It is good to obey God; and to believe in him; and to keep his commandments; and this is the life of man. And not to

obey God is evil, and this is his death. Since God gave much magnanimity, man knew both the good of obedience, and evil of disobedience, that the eye of the mind, receiving experience of both, may with judgment make choice of the better things; and that he may never become indolent or neglectful of God's command. Learning by experience that it is an evil thing which deprives him of life, that is, disobedience to God, he will never attempt it; but, knowing that what preserves his life, namely obedience to God, is good, he may keep it diligently and earnestly ... *Against Heresies,* 4.39[11]

It is the one and the same God, the Father, who has prepared good things with himself for those who desire his companionship, and who remain in subjection to him; and who has prepared the eternal fire for the ringleader of apostasy, the devil, and those who revolted with him ... *Against Heresies* 4.40[12]

In discussing the nature of man, Irenaeus described the foundations of the Church's moral teaching. For him, man was created as a child by God and put on trial. His perfection consists in the cultivation of the image of God within him, by means of the spirit that controls the actions of the will and moral conduct. The eternal existence of the soul depends upon man's conduct here, since man is not immortal by creation. He has been redeemed by Christ, and shares in this redemption through participation in the Church, and in her sacraments administered in the name of Christ. Through baptism, the new Adam is substituted for the old, for this sacrament renews the recapitulation of creation in Christ.

Irenaeus maintained that every man needs redemption and can receive it in Christ. Since the first parents fell and thereby subjected their descendants to sin and death, the Son of God has liberated mankind from the slavery of

[11]SC 100.
[12]SC 100. 947

Satan, sin and death. He has summed up the whole of creation in himself, and effected man's divine re-adoption and his reunion with God. In the second coming of Christ, mankind will be gathered together in Christ for the recapitulation or fulfillment of God's design in creation. Irenaeus does not say that man will be deified in his return to God but that he will adhere to God and participate in his glory.

> So the Word was made flesh that, through that very flesh which sin had ruled and dominated, sin should lose its force, and be no longer in us. Therefore our Lord took that same original formulation with his entry into our flesh, so that he might come near and do battle on behalf of the fathers, and conquer by Adam that which through Adam had stricken us down ... *Proof of the Apostolic Preaching* 31[13]

Irenaeus holds that the "natural laws" are the heart of all morality; that they were in existence before the "law of bondage" introduced by Moses. The Mosaic law was intended to force man, temporarily at least, to conform to God's will. With Christ's entrance into the world, the revelation of the "New Law" brought with it a renewal of man's true freedom. Once more man has a sure guide who is the original image of God - Christ, the head of the Church. It is only in the Church that man can work out his salvation, for there alone can he be assured of the divine truth on which to base his beliefs, and of divine grace that will lead him to the achievement of his true destiny.

> For the road of those who see is a single upward path, lighted by heavenly light; but the ways of those who see not, are many and dark and divergent. The former road leads to the kingdom of heaven by uniting man with God; but the others bring man down to death by severing him from God. Therefore must both you, and all those who

[13]SC 62. 81-82

look after the salvation of souls, make your way by faith, without deviation, but with courage and determination. Do not through lack of tenacity of perseverance remain at a standstill in material passions, or even be led astray, and turn aside from the straight path. *Apostolic Preaching*, [14]

2. Since man is an animal made up of soul and body, this renewal must come about through the instrumentality of both of these. Since occasions for stumbling come about from both of them, there is bodily holiness, that is safe-guarded by abstinence from all shameful things, and all wicked deeds; and a holiness of soul, by the preservation in its integrity of faith in God, adding nothing, and subtracting nothing from it.

For piety is clouded and loses its lustre by contamination and by impurity in the body; it is fractured, stained, and loses its integrity when falsehood enters the soul. But it will be preserved in beauty and measure by the constant abiding of truth in the mind, and of holiness in the body. For what is the use of knowing the truth in word, while defiling the body and accomplishing the works of evil? Or what real good can bodily holiness do, if truth be not in the soul? *Apostolic Preaching*[15]

There is an echo of the Two Ways in both this passage from the *Demonstration*, and in the passage quoted from *Against Heresies*. This moral teaching is an echo of Christ's admonitions: the stress on faith and reliance on the goodness of God who looks after man's welfare, and the call to progress, since tepidity is hateful to God. Irenaeus also stresses the holiness of the body, for he is attacking the dualistic Gnostics who held that material things were evil by their very nature. Even when the body is stained with impur-

[14]SC 62, 28
[15]SC 62, 29-31

ity, it does not become evil. On the other hand, when one preserves dignity and even integrity in his worldly actions, if he has not the humility of faith, such so-called bodily holiness is useless. Irenaeus insists with St. Paul that Christ put aside the Old Law of Moses as the pedagogue or moral guide for mankind. In the ancient educational system the pedagogue did not teach information or the arts; he guided the child's formation. Christ himself has become the pedagogue of mankind. He took the lessons taught by the Ten Commandments and reinterpreted them, showing that with the destruction of diabolical power through the redemption, a much holier and more highly spiritual conviction and way of life was possible. Irenaeus' commentary is dynamic and clever, intended to awaken an optimistic enthusiasm in his audience.

> Therefore we have no need of the law as a pedagogue. Behold we speak with the Father and stand face to face with him; we have become infants in evil doing; and we are made strong in all justice and propriety. For no more shall the law say: "Thou shalt not commit adultery," to him who has not even conceived the desire of another's wife; or "Thou shalt not kill," to him who has put away from himself all anger and enmity; or "thou shalt not covet thy neighbor's field, or his ox, or his ass," to those who make no account whatever of earthly things, but heap up profit in heaven. Nor "an eye for an eye and a tooth for a tooth," to him who counts no man his enemy, but all as his neighbors, and therefore cannot even put forth his hand to revenge. Nor will he demand titles of him who has vowed to God all his possessions, and who leaves father and mother and all his kindred, and follows the Word of God.
>
> Nor will he be commanded to set aside one day for rest, who is constantly keeping sabbath; that is, giving homage to God in the temple of God, which is man's body; and at all times doing the works of justice. "For I desire mercy,"

he says, "and not sacrifice; and the knowledge of God, more than holocausts." ... And no other name of the Lord has been given under heaven, whereby men are saved, but that of God who is Jesus Christ, the Son of God, whom even the devils obey, and the evil spirits, and all rebel powers. *Apostolic Preaching*, 96[16]

What is obvious in the total doctrine of Irenaeus as it has come down to present times is a double insistence. With Theophilus of Antioch he sees man originally created as a child. But that does not relieve him of responsibility. Even as a child, man was given the opportunity of asserting himself in accord with God's guidance or following his own capriciousness. When man chose to rebel against God's pedagogy because of his impatience, he received suitable treatment. Thus, Irenaeus insists again and again on man's liberty of conscience; and while he places equal weight upon responsibility, the latter has meaning only insofar as man enjoys the ability to pick and choose. This doctrine was a necessary teaching in the ancient world that was obsessed with fate and that saw a ruthless necessity (*anagké*) overpowering man in all his activities. One of the great blessings of Christianity was to spring the trap of the ancient teachings regarding fate, and by insisting upon man's free will and his liberty to make up his mind as he pleased - naturally suffering the consequences if he chose wrongly - to assert man's essential dignity as a free agent.

Irenaeus, on the other hand, had no patience with heresy either of a doctrinal variety or in moral matters. He saw vanity and arrogance (*hubris*) in the motivation of men who wanted to explain creation or the mysteries of the faith by introducing all kinds of mechanisms - like a complicated erector set or a Rube Goldberg illustration - between God

[16]SC 62, 163-165

and the world, between divine providence and man's use of grace. He vilified libertines who tried to cover up their perversities with mysterious theories about the soul, or blamed a god of evil instead of themselves for their wrongdoing.

Chapter Three

The Alexandrian Phase

In the fourth book of his *Ecclesiastical History*,[1] Eusebius of Caesarea describes a collection of letters written by Bishop Denis of Corinth during the pontificate of Pope Soter (166-175) that serve as an introduction to the development of the Church's moral teaching during the next five decades. Eusebius credits Denis with providing "catholic epistles" useful to the whole Church. To the Lacedimonians he has sent a catechesis devoted to peace and unity; to the Athenians, an exhortation to faith and conduct in keeping with the Gospel. Denis chided the Athenians for a loss of zeal, following the martyrdom of their Bishop, Publius, in 160 or 170, but encouraged them to rekindle their faith under their new Bishop, Quadratus. He sent the Church in Nicomedia a refutation of the dualism of Marcion and countered that heresy with the rule of true faith. To Crete he sent letters commending the Church's pilgrimaging at Gortyne as worthy of special praise for its cooperation in good deeds under its Bishop, Philip.

[1]SC 31. 202-206.

Writing to the churches of Amastris and of Pontus, in
Asia Minor, Denis speaks highly of their Bishop, Palmas. He
offered them counsel regarding marriage and continence,
and exhorted them to receive into communion repentant
sinners guilty of whatever fault, even of heresy. To Bishop
Pinytos of Cnossos, he suggested that the bishop should not
impose the heavy burden of continence on all the brethren
as a necessity, but that he should have consideration for the
weakness of the majority. In return, Denis received a letter
of acknowledgment in which Pinytos suggested that it
should be possible to instruct his people with stronger doctrine, lest, if they were continually milk-fed in the faith, they
would grow old conducting themselves like children. Commenting on this response, Eusebius suggests that Pinytos
thus gave indication of his keen understanding of divine
wisdom, and of his care for the progress of his people.
Finally, Eusebius quotes the letter of Denis to Soter of
Rome, in which the Bishop of Corinth praises the Roman
spirit of generosity in helping the indigent everywhere in the
Church, a trait characteristic of Rome from the beginning,
and that, as Eusebius remarks, persisted down to his own
day. Denis stated that, in its eucharistic gatherings on the
Day of the Lord, the Church of Corinth still read the Letter
of Clement of Rome, sent by way of admonition.

This information provides evidence of a considerable
development in the moral concerns of a large section of the
Church, as well as of a communal effort to prevent its
theological teaching from being undermined by heretics.
There is further indication that during this period the
Church experienced a vast expansion traceable, in part at
least, to the preaching of the Apologists, and in part to the
impression made by the steadfastness of the martyrs. With
this increase had come the inevitable necessity of reorganiz-
ing methods of instruction, and of strengthening the moral
fiber of both the faithful and the new arrivals. What is
somewhat peculiar is the fact that at Rome, at Alexandria in
Egypt, and at Carthage in North Africa, outstanding
churchmen suddenly emerge. They provide a theological
matrix for their respective churches that will have a funda-

mental bearing on the doctrinal and moral development of succeeding ages. Tertullian in Carthage, Hippolytus in Rome, and Clement in Alexandria almost simultaneously create theological patterns out of which a soteriological base for the church's moral doctrine will emerge in the course of the third century and greatly affect the moral and ethical teaching of the east and west down to the end of the patristic age.

Paradoxically it is to the pre-Christian theologian, Philo Judaeus of Alexandria (ca. 2 B.C.E. to 50 C.E.), that one should look in an attempt to discover the fundamental elements of this partistic heritage. Philo provides the bridge between the Judeo-Hellenic and the Christian metaphysical system and he accomplishes this task with decisiveness. He insists, to begin with, that the supreme being adored by the Jews is nameless, thus indescribable and transcendent. In so doing, he liberates the Christian theology of the future from attachment to any particular metaphysical system. This is exactly the fact that will be acknowledged by Tertullian in his startling challenge, *Quid Athenis Hierosolymis* - what has Jerusalem to do with Athens? (*De Praescriptione Haereticorum*, 7, 9).

Philo himself was strictly eclectic in his philosophical adherence. He combined a depth of critical appreciation of Plato with a large acceptance of the Stoic and the Aristotelian logic. And this mind set he handed on to his Christian *epigones*.

Philo's primary achievement was a vast *Commentary on the Pentateuch* that can be considered a fundamental accomplishment of the Hebraic wisdom. He approaches the Book of Genesis as, in Henry Chadwick's phrase, "a cosmic cryptogram." In it Moses had concealed an all-embracive metaphysical system whereby he described the origin and the actuality of the cosmos including the creation of mankind. It included a complete ethical code under the guise of creational myths, the Jewish patriarchal narratives, and the ceremonial laws. Philo uses a diagnostic method to explain the mosaic cosmogony while elucidating the true significance of the prophets and the law. In explaining the Old

Testament mysteries, he employs the allegorical methods with which the Greek philosophers had interpreted Homer and the myths of the ancient gods, to undercut the criticism and allay the ridicule directed at the anthropomorphism of the earlier theogonies.

In the hellenistic synagogues of the diaspora in the centers of Greek civilization, the older teachers had expended considerable energy on praising the hoary antiquity of Moses and the ancient Jewish culture. In relation to this longevity, Philo maintained that Plato and the Greek philosophers had read the Old Testament and were reflecting the wisdom that Moses and the prophets had hidden under the guise of law and the preaching of the prophets to avoid the problem of attributing to the divinity the cause of evil.

He employs the two stories of creation in *Genesis* (1-2:3 and 2:4-25) to excellent advantage. The description of the creation in seven days that occupies the first chapter of *Genesis* is made the equivalent of Plato's conception of the world of ideas. This first creation was non-material and non-spatial; it existed in the *logos* or divine reason as in an architect's plan which was unfolded at first in the Creator's mind, without consideration of time or location. Hence, the "days" of this creation represent merely order within the ideal world. Man is identified as a manifestation of the divine reasoning power through which he is the "image of God." Finally, Philo, following Plato, conceded that the Creator had used secondary causes - angels or daimones - in structuring the cosmos in order.

When he took up the second story of creation in *Genesis*, Philo asserted that here God respected the limitations engendered by time and space. The first man now is a combination of matter and spirit made from mother earth, but containing the image of God breathed into him by the *logos*. He is distinctively male, and a citizen of the world, a summation of the created universe, or a *microcosmos*. He is the very true king of all time. But his downfall began with the creation of woman who emphasized the material part of his nature, particularly awakening in him physical desire.

Philo's God is the personal God of Abraham, Isaac and Jacob. But he is also the transcendental superior being of whom all that is known is that "He is." His Jewish monotheism absorbed both the Stoic conception of immanent divine power as a vital force in the universe, and the Platonic transcendence of the supra-cosmic supreme being. From the Pythagoreans he obtained a feeling for a cryptic symbolism in the sensible world that he sees as a constantly changing reflection of the intelligent order in the universe, and a justification for his allegorical interpretation of poetic myth, gnomic morality, and the advocacy of *enkrateia* or self-control as a preparation of immortality.

Philo's approach to the problem of evil is syncretistic. Inherent in being created is the fact of being "fallen" - hence, sinfulness is congenital with human nature. Not merely is man subject to moral disorder because he is finite, but he is also the victim of pride in the desire to be equal to God that is the root of sin. Philo combines this Mosaic reflection with the Platonic myth of the souls who had lost their wings after becoming sated with the divine goodness in the *Phaedrus*. He sees some of these souls used as angels - or the daimones of the pagans - and others as mortal men. The fact that inferior angels shared in creation explains the origin of evil that can in no way be imputed to God. In the long run, evil, whether physical or moral, is the result of disorder of its very nature and is thus below the divine being.

Philo's ethic of perfection is likewise a crossing of Jewish and hellenic disciplines. During the span of his earthly life, he says, man here is a pilgrim. Like Abraham he must migrate from the astral religion of Ur of the Chaldees to the true religion of the promised land. In the course of its wanderings, the human soul must achieve a spiritual self-discipline and come to understand that the body, though good in itself, is the main obstacle to perfection. Thus, the way of salvation opens through an act of faith like that of Abraham. It demands a determination by the will to restrain unreasoning lusts of the flesh and to advance beyond the moderation counselled by Aristotle to the complete *apatheia* demanded by the Stoics.

This discipline is the proper preparation for the mystical contemplation of God that, as St. Paul will demonstrate, is a "seeing and being seen" by the invisible godhead. This achievement is beyond reasoning since God is unknowable. Philo, thus, enters the *via negativa* theology and arrives at the dilemma posed by mystical experience. To this problem he contributes a remarkable commentary on the need for grace as both revelation and the enabling power whereby man must rise above moralism to contemplation and achieve a knowledge of himself by losing himself in the supreme being.

Philo's fate was connected with the rise of Christianity, of which he knew nothing. There is little trace of his influence on talmudic Judaism, and no mention of him among the medieval Jewish philosophers. While his exegetical ideas anticipate much of the thought of St. Paul, St. John, and the Epistle to Hebrews, it is only with the third century Alexandrian theologians, Clement and Origen, that he comes into his own.

Attempts to trace direct Philonic influences in the New Testament and on the early Apologists from Tatian and Justin to Irenaeus and Tertullian have aborted. When these primitive Christian authors parallel Philo in dealing with cognate materials, they are evidently drawing from similar sources. Beginning with the early Alexandrian fathers, however, the Philonic influence is direct, deep and extensive.

Clement of Alexandria

Immediately dependent on Philo for his attitude toward reason and revelation is the first of the great Greek Christian theologians, Clement of Alexandria, who died ca. 215. Clement was a philosopher and a Christian convert who succeeded Pantaenus as a *didaskalos* or teacher in explaining and defending the Christian philosophy at Alexandria. Nothing is known of his birth, background or education. In his writings, he attempted to assuage the fears of simple believers, while satisfying the gnostic esotericism of the educated Christians and repelling the attacks of cultured critics who despised the new religion as a return to barbarism. In four principal works, the *Protrepticus* or Invitation/Challenge to prospective converts, the *Pedagogus*, or Teacher, the eight books of the *Stromateis* or theological miscellanies, and his *Quis dives salvetur*? (*What rich man will be saved?*) - he gives a thorough explanation of the Christian way of life.

> Instruction in conformity with Christ teaches that God the Creator has caused his providence to extend down to the minutest details. It understands that the nature of the world's material elements are constantly changing and being created. It learns from its guide the manner in which it can resemble God and proclaim the divine plan (economy) as principal director of all instruction. *Str.* 1.11.52, 3[2]

Following Philo, Clement maintains that philosophy prepares the soul for divine knowledge just as music, geometry and astronomy train the mind for philosophy. It enables the understanding to rise above material horizons and grasp abstract notions. Clement is more interested in epistemology than Philo as he builds up a body of information in his *Stromateis* that starts with an inquiry into the way of defining the nature of religious assent and justifying speculative reason as essential to the proper grasp of faith. He insists that there is no escape from the use of philosophy, not merely in refuting heresy and ridicule, but in explaining central matters of Christian doctrine.

> Before the coming of the Lord, philosophy served the Greeks as a necessary path to justification. It is now an inducement to piety, an exercise in training for those who come to the faith by way of argumentation. "For you will not lose your footing" it is said, "if you attribute all that is good among us or the Hellenes to Providence ..."

[2]SC 30, 87.

> Apparently, philosophy was given to the Greeks prima-
> rily for their direction until the Lord should call them. It
> was a school-master striving to bring the Hellenic mind to
> Christ as the Law was for the Hebrews. Philosophy was
> consequently a preparation paving the way for him who
> achieves perfection in Christ. *Str.* 1.5.28[3]

Clement stands squarely on the doctrine of creation as the
beginning of both reality and of the knowledge of what
exists. All truth and goodness are from God, and Christ is
the embodiment of what is known as the Way, the Truth,
and the Life. God gave the Jews the Old Testament as a
tutor. He furnished the Greeks with philosophy to lead them
to an appreciation of divine wisdom. But Clement agrees
with Philo that the Greeks had originally stolen their wisdom from Moses; and he assumes Philo's contention that
the two accounts of creation in *Genesis* describe the origin
first of the intelligible universe - hence of souls, angelic,
human and demonic - and then of the sensible world. The
image of God in *Genesis* (1:26f) is the divine Logos who is
thus the archetype of the human mind.

Clement maintains that creation was an experiment in
freedom emanating from God's goodness and love in which
the Creator gives to beings that derive from the divine will
the opportunity not only to be separate from their Creator,
but to exercise an innate freedom to love or to repel their
Maker. In tracing the origin of man and his universe to
God's will, rather than to the divine essence, Clement again
emphasizes the fact that the material world was made out of
nothing; that its essence is good; and that there was no room
for the crudities of anthropomorphism in man's concept of
the creator.

Clement's philosophical system is a type of middle Plato-
nism that he recognizes as having consciously fused Plato's
metaphysical system with Stoic ethics and Aristotelian
logic. He rejects the notion that the cosmos is eternal or that
the universe was created in time. He sees the stars as made

[3]SC 30, 65,

primarily to indicate the passage of time, and asserts that if they have any influence on human affairs, it is put there by God.

In the *Protrepticus* or Invitation, Clement had explained that the "image of God" is his Logos - a truly divine person because he is the Son of God, the archetype and the light of light - in whose likeness the spirit of man was created with intelligence and reason. He then extended the notion of God's philanthropy or love of man to embrace the whole of mankind, thus guaranteeing the fact that what the pagan philosophers, poets and legislators had achieved in striving for goodness was supported by God's providence. "Homer prophetizes without knowing it," he says; and Plato, "talks like a disciple of the Word." He finds that Sophocles and Pindar are disciples of Moses.

According to ancient usage, the pedagogue was a servant, usually a slave, who attended a child as a nurse, guide, exactor of studies and protector against the physical and moral dangers to be met with outside the home. In his book, the *Pedagogue*, Clement uses this concept to portray the Logos or Christ conducting the Christian to a knowledge and practice of virtue on his way to perfection.

To achieve this Way of Life, God's stimulus or grace is essential. It is present from the start in as far as man is created in God's image, modelled on Christ who is the perfect, personal reflection of the Father as the godhead.

By his intemperate desire to achieve knowledge and experience, man has behaved as a wilful child and thus gravely obscured the resemblance of God in which he is created. He has been deceived by false goods, mainly through misrepresentation placed before him by evil spirits. To remedy his errors, he needs the guidance of a pedagogue who will correct his evil tendencies, teach him how to control his passions, gradually heal the wounds inflicted on him by his sins, and assist him in understanding the word of God placed before him by the divine teacher or pedagogue.

In the composition of this book, Clement's primary source, unacknowledged, is the Roman Stoic writer, C. Musonius Rufus, the teacher of Epictetus. A major portion

of the descriptive material in the *Pedagogue* is taken, sometimes verbatim, from Musonius Rufus' Diatribe. Sections
on woman's place in society, sexual morality, the purpose
behind marriage, on nutrition, clothing, grooming, and the
household are lifted directly with their pertinent examples
and maxims: "one should eat to live, not live to eat;" and in
the matter of sexual activity, "follow nature" means that
conjugal relations are to be indulged only for the sake of
procreating children.

> Embracing more and more a healthy obedience, we hand
> ourselves over to the Lord in knowing that man and
> woman have the same virtue. If there is but one God for
> both of them, there is but one Pedagogue, one Church,
> one moderation and temperance, one modesty, a com-
> mon table, married love, breathing, obedience, charity: in
> all things they are equal. Who have a common life, they
> have a common grace and a common salvation; and
> theirs is a common edification and love. *Pedagogue* 4, 10,
> 1[4]

Descending to the particulars of taste and customs, Clement advises that only what is truly civilized is ethically
acceptable and can lead to the nobility of life that becomes a
gnostic Christian. Self-mastery is the ideal that motivates
the Christian art of living. Rejected in this scheme of ethics
are the vices of *hubris* (arrogance) and softness (*truphe*) that
destroy men and civilizations. In their place, the Christian
should cultivate frugality and simplicity leading through
self-control to *ataraxia* or total self-mastery, the goal of
earthly human existence.

Within this framework, Clement inserts a biblical ethic.
Thus, in the chapter on sexual morality, he insists that the
couple in procreating obey the divine command "Increase
and multiply" and, thus, participate in a demiurgic power by
bringing into being another Image of God.

[4]SC 70, 129.

While some Christians are destined for a celibate life, it is wrong to regard celibacy as closer to God than the married state. Sexual intercourse in no way signifies a moral or ritual defilement. In fact, the married man has greater opportunity for holiness than the celibate: in everyday life the griefs he must endure from wife, children and household chores.

Echoing the Stoics and Plato, Clement insists that conjugal relations are for the begetting of children, not for self-indulgence. Hence, married love requires restraint and respect. Excess or satiety can destroy love.

While the universe is anthropocentric, and all things are created for the use of man, man is in turn created for the service of God. While all worldly goods should be shared in common, Clement insists that the basis of this communitarianism should rise from the community of nature to the evangelical concept of the love of one's neighbor - from the *koinonikon* to the *agapelikon*. The Epicurean axiom, "No one should lack what is necessary," is turned toward the "knowledge of God" and the Aristotelian counsel, "Live as free men, not as slaves," calls for a liberation from the slavery of sin. Vanity of all kinds indulged by men and women is considered as insulting to God's provisions for man's well-being and beauty, and, thus, an indulgence in an *antidemiourgein* - against one's function as a demiurge.

In his *Quis dives salvetur?* - (*What rich man will be saved?*) - Clement interprets Christ's admonition to the rich young man to sell all he has and give it to the poor as a command to strip the soul of its passions.

> What he (Christ) enjoins is new and peculiar to God and alone life-giving. In "the new creation," the Son of God reveals something unique. His command does not refer to the visible act, what others have done, but to something grander—to strip the soul itself and the will of their lurking passions. It is possible for a person after having unburdened himself of his property to be nonetheless absorbed in the desire and longing for it. For when a person lacks the necessities of life, he cannot fail to be

broken in spirit and neglect the higher things as he strives
to obtain these necessities by any means and from any
source.

And how much more useful is the opposite condition
when by possessing what is sufficient a man is himself in
no distress about money-making and is able to help those
whom he should assist. And how could this teaching be
found other than plainly at war with other noble doctrines of the Lord? How could we feed the hungry and
give drink to the thirsty, cover the naked and shelter the
homeless ... if we lacked those things? 12-13.[5]

In the second and third books of the *Pedagogue*, Clement
describes the moral motivation that accompanies the Christian during the full course of the day. It commences with the
evening meal, the sole true repast of the ancient world. He,
thus, gives admonitions for the proper manner of eating and
drinking, and the genteel conduct that becomes the symposium that follows the meal, as well as the use of flowers,
perfumes and festive ornaments. Entering the bed chamber,
he gives the rules for sleep, then discusses sexual morality
beginning with the process for the procreation of infants
which he maintains is the sole proper end of marriage.

Book III is devoted to a satire on feminine coquetry (ii)
and masculine vanity (III), as well as a description of man's
daily activities from his treatment of domestics and animals
(iv), the use of the public baths and physical exercise (v and
vi) to the discourse against luxury and on the proper use of
riches (vii and viii). In conclusion, Clement gives a summation of his moral thought together with a diatribe against
public spectacles and a Hymn to Christ the Savior.

Clement's indispensible service to the Church and Christian civilization did not receive the recognition it deserved
down to modern times. As a pioneer and predecessor of
Origen, his orthodoxy was questioned, thus denying him the
designation of a saint.

[5]PG 9, 616-17.

Origen (184-254)

Of Origen, Clement's successor as the Alexandrian theologian, much more is known biographically due to the tumultuous nature of his career as a Christian pedagogue and prophet and the voluminous character of his writings. Nor is his subsequent fate without interest. In 202, at age 18, he replaced his martyred father, Leonidas, as the head of the household and started a private school in Alexandria for the family's sustenance. To acquaint himself with Greek philosophy, he studied under Ammonius Saccas, the ex-Christian teacher of Plotinus.

Selected by Bishop Demetrios of Alexandria as his catechist and eventually theologian, Origen evidently ran a school for converts more like an open forum than an academic establishment. Later he fell from the good graces of his bishop when he accepted ordination to the priesthood from Bishop Theoctistus of Palestine where he had been engaged as an official preacher despite the fact that he was still a layman.

Origen travelled widely at the expense of well-to-do admirers interested in Christianity. He visited Cappadocia and Arabia, brought Bishop Beryllus of Bostra back to orthodoxy, and studied church traditions in both Greece and Rome. In Caesarea, he was instrumental in adding to the great Christian library started there by the martyr, Pamphilus. Meanwhile, he devoted himself to obtaining an authentic version of the scriptures, composing large-scale commentaries on the Old and New Testaments, as well as to the refutation of attacks of learned pagans directed against the church and its teachings. Through his pupil, Gregory Thaumaturgus (the Wonder Worker), who wrote a panegyric describing Origen's teaching methods and scholarly program, he had great influence on the Cappadocians of the next century. Two of them, Basil and Gregory of Nazianzus, have been credited with publishing the anthology of Origen's theological opinions, known as the *Philocalia,* that had great influence on Greek and Byzantine spirituality down to modern times.

Eusebius of Caesarea devotes part of the Sixth Book of his *Church History* to Origen, whom he calls Adamantius, or Man of Steel, for his ascetical practices and straightforward thinking.

> He persevered, as far as possible, in a philosopher's manner of life. At one time, he disciplined himself by fasting. At another, he measured out the time for sleep which he carefully took, not on a bed or couch, but on the floor. Above all, he considered that the sayings of the Savior in the Gospel exhorting us not to possess two coats nor use shoes, nor be worn out with worries about the future, should be followed strictly. *Eccl. Hist.* 6. 3, 9-11[6]

Eusebius reveals one secret behind Origen's prodigious literary accomplishments when he describes the atmosphere in which he worked.

> Origen's commentaries on the scriptues had their start at the instigation of Ambrose (a rich Alexandrian whom Origen had converted to Christianity). This man not only presented him with countless exhortations and encouragements, but supplied him unstintingly with all the things necessary for his work. As he dictated, there were on hand seven shorthand writers who relieved each other at stated times, and a like number of copyists as well as girls skilled in calligraphy. All of these people were supplied the necessary materials by Ambrose. *Eccl. Hist.* 6.23.1-2[7]

Origen gives a synthetic overview of the Christian faith in his treatise, *On First Principles.* It is not a true *summa theologica*, but rather a reasoned refutation of the gnostic ideology so prevalent in the religious atmosphere of the day. He begins by stating the fundamental teachings of the

[6]SC 41, 89.
[7]SC 41, 123.

Church as they have been received and handed down by the apostles. These doctrines are to be believed by both the simple and learned faithful without question.

> All who believe and are assured that grace and truth were obtained through Jesus Christ, and who know Christ to be the Truth, in keeping with his assurance, "I am the Truth," derive the knowledge that leads mankind to a good and happy life from no other source than from the words and teachings of Christ. *On First Principles, Preface*[8]

Acknowledging the fact that among believers in Christ there were both trifling and grave differences in their concepts of divine truth, even about God, the Lord Jesus Christ and the Holy Spirit, Origen felt constrained to outline the rule of faith before approaching doctrines he considered open to speculation.

> It should be stated that the holy apostles, when preaching the faith in Christ, made themselves totally clear on matters they believed necessary to all believers even those who were dull in their apprehension of divine truth. However, they left the reasons behind their enunciations open to examination by those who, through the grace of the Spirit, had the gifts of language, wisdom and knowledge ... to examine their meanings and manner of origin. *Ibid 3*[9]

Origen's basic distinction between the essentials of the faith and matters open to discussion did not spare him the accusation of heresy that adhered to his works down through the centuries. This accusation began while he was still alive. It was renewed at the turn of the fifth century; and he was condemned by the Council of Constantinople II in

[8]SC 252, 76.
[9]SC 252, 78.

553 under Justinian. Nevertheless, his importance in the development of the Christian theology was immense, particularly in the West where his works were translated into Latin and used extensively, frequently under pseudonyms making the rediscovery of many of his writings difficult.

A prodigious author, Origen sought out the ancient Hebrew and Greek texts of the scriptures to provide the church with an authentic version of the Word of God. He produced innumerable homilies and commentaries on both the Old and New Testaments. And he wrote tracts on martyrdom, prayer, and on Truth against Celsus.

Origen goes much further than Philo and Clement in his allegorical interpretation of the scriptures, adding a search for a moral and anagogic, or eschatological sense, to the literal and spiritual meaning acknowledged by his predecessors. In his preface to the *On First Principles*, he gives the basis for his interpretations.

> By the words of Christ we do not mean those only which he spoke when he became man and was housed in the flesh. Before that time, Christ the Word of God was in Moses and the prophets. For without the Word of God how could they have been able to prophesy in Christ? Were it not our intention to restrict this treatise within the confines of brevity, it would not be difficult to prove this statement by showing in the sacred scriptures how Moses and the prophets spoke and performed all they did through being filled with the spirit of Christ. *On First Principles: Preface*[10]

In his various commentaries and sermons, he searches each text for the presence of the Logos that is Christ who, as the Alpha and Omega, must be everywhere present in God's Word as it is captured in the Bible. Origen's *Contra Celsum*, the pagan philosopher whose treatise on Truth (*Aletheia*) was a highly intelligent attack against Christianity by one

[10]SC 252, 76.

who had read all the literature and observed the behavior of Christians, is one of the great pieces of Christian apologetic. Accepting the accusation that he is borrowing from Greek literature to adorn the Christian message, Origen attempts to refute Celsus on the writer's own terms. While Clement of Alexandria had taken a subtle delight in the fact that upon becoming a Christian the arrogant Greek had to bow before the barbarian (Jewish and Christian) wisdom, Origen rejects the charge that Christianity is a return to a type of barbarism and superstition.

He repudiates the idea that the anthropomorphic description of God in the Scriptures can be taken literally. He traces the continuity of the history of man's salvation from the primitive revelation to Adam and Eve through the Hebrew experience down to the coming of Christ the Redeemer. He maintains that Christ was either seminally present or foreshadowed in all that went before, and insists that Christianity is a religion of courage and enterprise not unlike the vision that inspired the heroes of old, such as Ulysses and Odysseus to set out on their journeys of adventure. Nevertheless, he does not want the Christian to get involved in imperial politics or in all-encompassing secular affairs. He informs Celsus that Christians do more for the empire and its rulers by their prayers than they could possibly do in the army or administrative services.

> As we by our prayers vanquish the demons who stir up war and lead to the violation of oaths, disturbing the peace, we are much more useful to the emperors than those who take to the field to fight for them. We do participate in public affairs, when along with righteous prayers, we join self-denying exercises and meditations that teach us to despise pleasures . . . none fight better for the emperor than we do . . . forming a special army of piety by offering our prayers to God. *Against Celsus* 8.7-3[11]

[11]SC 150, 346.

In his moral teaching, Origen puts a metaphysical foundation beneath his doctrine in *On First Principles*: 3, 6, 1[12].

> The highest good, to which every rational nature hastens, is also called the "end of all that is" even by many philosophers who maintain that the highest good is to become, as far as possible, similar to God. This, however, is not a discovery of the others (pagans) for I believe it has been taken from our divine books. For Moses asserts: "Let us make man in our own image and likeness." Then he adds, "and God did make man, and in the image of God he made him." Gen.

> The fact that in this last sentence the prophet speaks of God making man in his "image," but is select about his "likeness" means nothing less than that man received the dignity of the divine image in his original condition. The perfection of God's likeness was delayed for the end so that man himself might achieve it through the efforts of his striving to imitate God. He then had a possiblity of perfecting himself that was granted in the beginning through the dignity of the divine image. In the end, through the exertion of his efforts, he might achieve for himself a perfect likeness to God.

> Hence, we must inquire diligently what is this perfection of beatitude and the end of all things, when we say that, not only is God in all things, but is all in all things.

Origen attempted to go deeper into the interstices of human behavior, insisting uncompromisingly on human free will over against a powerful segment of the philosophy of his day that saw nothing new under the sun and gave a cyclic explanation of human existence, thus abolishing the notion of progress. Reaching back to Plato via Philo and Clement, he makes good use of the twofold story of creation

[12]SC 269.

in Genesis. He maintains that in the beginning God created intelligences bunched around the supreme Intelligence of the Godhood; and that, when they failed in their total attention to the divine being, the second creation, that of the universe, was necessitated to supply a material locale for the angels, human beings and the devils who were deprived of the immediate divine presence.

Continuing this theological reflection on man's moral destiny, Origen maintains:

> God dispenses minds not only for the brief space of this life that spans sixty or a few more years, but for a perpetual and eternal time. Just as he is immortal and eternal, God holds out a similar provision for immortal souls. For he has made a rational nature capable of being incorruptible when he created it to his own image and likeness. (13.274-5)[13]

Dealing with the pragmatic aspects of the daily life of the early Christians, Origen describes the efforts made by itinerant philosophers, cynics and other wandering preachers to gather disciples and teach them a way of life in keeping with the dictates of a love of humanity. He contrasts their ways with the Christian invitation to conversion leading to baptism and entrance into the Christian assembly or church. He recounts the scrutiny of the catechumens for their sincerity and conversion to a new way of life.

> We convert young women from impurities, from battling with their husbands, from the insanity of the theatre and dancing halls, from superstitions of all kinds ... young men and boys from lasciviousness and the wild doings of Venus ... warning them not only of a bad reputation but of the punishment that will follow.

> Since we know that many saints, even among the apostles, were married, we cannot think that holiness belongs

only to virginity ... While there is a gradation (in holiness) whereby after the apostles come the first class of martyrs, then of virgins, then of the continent ... I do not think that the married who abstain for a time for prayer and in all things act in a holy manner and justly, cannot be among those who present themselves as a "living host," holy and pleasing to God, nor are virgins and the continent such, if they are soiled by the vice of pride, or avarice, or a wicked tongue, or the evils of falsehoods. *Against Celsus* 3[14]

Concerned with the psychological elements involved in human sinfulness, Origen draws on his own experience in dealing with the everyday behavior of Christians and others. He set out this information with the lessons and admonitions on daily life preserved in the scriptures. He then produced a theory of human behavior that is both spiritually and pragmatically valid.

Divine scripture teaches us that there are certain invisible enemies fighting against us. It commands that we arm ourselves against them. Hence the more simple among those believing in the Lord Christ think that all the sins that human beings commit are the result of the urging of the mind to wrong doing by these contrary powers. Thus (they say) that if there were no devil, no human being would commit evil. ... But just as the devil is not the cause of our hunger and thirst, so he is not the cause of the movements that naturally occur to the adult, namely the desire of enjoying sexual intercourse. It is certain that it is not always the devil who causes these movements. Hence, it must not be thought that without the devil bodies would not experience the desire for such involvements. I am certain that in all the other natural movements of the soul a similar situation prevails, namely in cupidity,

[14]SC 136, 133.

wrath, sorrow and in all the things where the vice of intemperance exceeds the measure of the natural way of doing things. *On First Principles* 3, 2, 1-2[15]

Origen further describes the mental and emotional processes:

It is evident then that, as in doing good, human propensity by itself is not adequate for the achievement of its end, it is led by divine assistance to its accomplishment; so, on the contrary, we receive the initial impulse, and as it were, the seed of sinfulness from the things that are natural to our experience. When, therefore, "we indulge ourselves beyond what is sufficient" and do not resist the first movements of intemperance, thus accepting the impulse of this primary defect, then hostile forces urge and strive in every which way to enlarge sinfulness and present to human beings occasion and initiation in sin ... Thus, a fall into avarice is brought about, when, at first, people desire only a little money, then the vice increases and cupidity takes over. After this blindness of mind follows passion and inimical forces suggest and stimulate convetousness., No more merely desired, it is taken by force or conquered by the shedding of human blood. A similar process is experienced when the vexations of the devils are experienced in immoderate lovemaking, the intemperance of anger, or the indulgence of depression (306-307) *On First Principles, Ibid.*[16]

Origen gives a further consideration to this most important principle:

Since in our apostolic preaching there is belief in the future judgment of a just God, the believability of this judgment provokes and persuades mankind to live well

[15]SC 269.
[16]SC 269.

and virtuously, fleeing all kinds of sin. For in this manner is indicated doubtlessly that it is in our power to lead either a praiseworthy or an unacceptable life. Hence, I deem it necessary to say something about the freedom of the will. *On First Principles* 3, 1, 1[17]

The thoughts that proceed from within our hearts and the memory of the past deeds sometimes come from within us; sometimes they are suggested by contrary spirits; sometimes they are intimated by God or his angels. This fact might seem improbable were it not confirmed by Sacred Scripture ... Indeed, the book of the Shepherd Hermas confirms it by speaking of the angels who accompany every human being: the good angel and the bad angel ... This is also the message of the Letter of Barnabas speaking of the "two ways" with the two angels, one of light and one of darkness.

Nevertheless, we have the ability, when evil spirits incite us to do evil, to cast from us their wicked suggestions and resist evil persuasion and do nothing culpable. Again, it is possible when divine powers incite us to do better things and we do not follow, thus preserving in us the power of free will. *On First Principles* 3, 2, 4[18]

Regarding penance and the remission of sins, Origen has a very positive doctrine, though he does nothing to resolve modern questions regarding the nature of the confession of sins and absolution in the early church.

Some of the faithful may say, "It would be better to do as our ancestors among the Jews and pagans did when with sacrifices made in varying rites they received pardon of their sins." With us, however, there is only one pardon for sin, namely the grace of baptism in the beginning. After

[17]SC 269.
[18]SC 269.

this there is no mercy for the sinner nor any forgiveness given. It is proper that Christians, for whom Christ died, to have a stricter discipline. *Homily in Lev.* 2, 4[19]

As this intransigent stand was of little use or consolation to the post-baptismal sinner, Origen concedes that in God's sight sinners of all kinds were continually receiving pardon.

> Listen then to the many ways for the forgiveness of sins given in the Gospels. The first is baptism with its remission of sins; the second forgiveness comes through the sufferings of the martyrs; the third is by way of almsgiving; the fourth is the remission of our sins when we forgive those who sin against us; the fifth when we bring someone who is a sinner back from the error of his ways; the sixth by a super abundance of charity as our Lord said: "Her sins are forgiven her because she loved much." And there is finally a seventh way, but it is laborious and difficult; namely, the remission of sins through penance. When the sinner washes his spirit with his tears and his tears are with him day and night; and when he does not blush to tell his sin to the Lord's priest and seek the remedy. *Homily in Lev.* 2, 4[20]

Origen deals with the transmission of sinfulness in his Homily on Lev. 8, 3[21].

> Listen to David when he says, "I was conceived in iniquity and in sin my mother bore me." This proves that every soul born in the flesh is tainted with the stain of iniquity and sin. For this reason, we say (with Job) that no human being is free of sinfulness, not even if he be but one day in life. To this consideration may be added the inquiry as to

[19]SC 286, 106-108.
[20]SC 286, 108.
[21]SC 287, 21.

> why, since baptism in the church is given for the remission of sins, it is the custom of the Church to administer baptism even to infants.

Origen supplied the answer to this question in his Homily on Romans 5.9 by asserting that the custom of infant baptism was handed down by the apostles. He maintains that these men were entrusted with the secrets of the divine mysteries. Hence, they knew that infants were tainted with the taint of original sin and needed to be washed in water and the spirit. He makes no reference to the Virgin Mary in this avowal nor of the doctrine of her immaculate conception that will trouble the next generation. Nor does he give a clear-cut picture of the practice of the forgiveness of sin and reconciliation in the Church of third century Alexandria. In his *On Prayer* he provides a commentary on the "Our Father" in which he describes at length the petition "forgive us our trespasses or debts" without discussing the sacramental structure of the penitential practice. He does, however, refer to the problem of the sins after baptism that the early Church, for the most part, considered irremissible, a problem highlighted by Tertullian and the African church, in particular.

> I fail to understand how some men arrogate to themselves a power greater than the sacerdotal dignity. Perhaps they do not have an accurate grasp of the knowledge proper to a priest. Hence, they boast they can forgive adultery and remit sins of idolatry and fornication. They act as if through their prayer for those who have dared to commit such crimes, even the sin unto death were forgiven. *On Prayer* 28.10[22]

While Origen provides no answer this side of eternity, he has no such doubts about the remission of all sinfulness in the *apoktastasis* or return of all that exists into the Godhead.

[22]Cf Origen, *On Prayer*, ACW 19, 112-113.

The end of the world and the final consummation will take place when everyone will have been subjected to punishment for sins. It is a time that God alone knows when he will bestow on each one what he deserves. We think indeed that God's goodness through his Christ may recall all his creatures to one final conclusion when even his enemies will be conquered and subdued ...

Stronger than all the evils in the soul is the Word and the healing power that dwells within him. This healing he applies to everyone in keeping with God's will. Thus, the consummation of all things implies the destruction of evil ... *Against Celsus* 8.72 [23]

For his optimistic view that even the devils might be converted and all evil annihilated at the end of time, Origen was condemned as heretical. But the legacy of his teaching concerning mankind's moral structure has affected the Church's doctrine most positively down through the ages.

Methodius of Olympus

Paradoxically the man known as one of Origen's most damaging critics, Methodius of Olympus, had been among his earliest imitators. Little is known of the late third century author of the *Symposium* or Dialogue on Virginity other than what can be gleaned from its contents. They point to a Platonically oriented Christian with Aristotelian sensitivity; an author of considerable secular and religious learning, steeped in the early church's theological traditions. Jerome, in his *Illustrious Men*, describes him as bishop of Olympus in Greece and cites him as a martyr in either 303 or 311 A.D. As he is not described in the *Ecclesiastical History* of Eusebius, little further authentic information is available.

[23]SC 150, 340-346.

Besides the *Symposium*, Methodius wrote a tract *On Free Will*, a Dialogue on the Resurrection called *Aglaophon* and a number of other treatises—*On Life*, *On Food*, *On Created Things*—only sections of which have been preserved.

In the *Symposium*, a Platonic dialogue in eleven sectors, Methodius displays considerable erudition as well as an Origenistic allegorical method without acknowledgment. In the *Aglaophon*, Methodius turns out to be Origen's earliest and severest critic who rejects his notion of a double creation—of intellects first, then the material universe—but seems to be only partly aware of the in-depth problems Origen confronted in his effort to free Christianity and the Creator of responsibility for bringing evil and the devil into existence.

While concentrating on chastity as the greatest of the Christian virtues, Methodius supplies what might be considered a compendium of the Christian Way of Life. In the course of eleven discourses, he gives practical instruction on the nature of the allegorical interpretation of the Scriptures; on the divinity of Christ; the meaning of world history; the nature of the millenium and the concept of eternity. He offers practical advice on interpreting Paul's Epistles, on prayer, the method of combating temptation, the freedom of the will and the fallacy of astrology.

These interests had been raised in what seems to have been the first of his compositions, *On Free Will*, in which he dealt with the problem of evil by denying that sin is the result of man's or the universe's material composition. Matter, he maintains, created by God, is good in itself.

In the *Symposium*, Methodius contends that virginity or continence is the answer to Plato's *Eros* as mankind's fundamental ideal. He, thus, combines Platonic notions with the teaching of St. Paul on marriage and virginity.

> Great beyond measure, admirable and glorious is virginity... Reflecting directly the mind and meaning of the sacred scriptures, it is rich in incorruption. It is a beauti-

ful and noble way of life... Chastity is rare among mankind and a goal difficult of attainment... *Symposium* 1.1 [24]

The foundation of Methodius' moral teaching is the Church, not only considered in its existential actuality, but in its ideal conception in the mind of God.

As the body of Christ, the Church was in existence from the creation; it had a potential though hidden form in the Old Testament and achieved actuality in the world with the birth of Christ. In its activities it betrays a charismatic modality through the action of the Holy Spirit. *Ibid.*

Stressing the divine involvement with the human,

The words 'increase and multiply' are daily fulfilled in the Church as it grows day by day in size and beauty and numbers, thanks to the intimate union between it and the world. He came down to distribute his ecstasy among us by the memorial of his passion. Otherwise the Church could not conceive and bring forth the faithful by the laver of regeneration (baptism) ... He came down from heaven to die and then to cling to his spouse the Chruch allowing a power to be removed from his side by which act mankind could grow strong in the spirit. Discourse 3.8.[25]

The substance of Methodius' theological concern is captured in his description of the history of mankind seen from a divine perspective. It revolves round creation, the fall, the redemption and man's restoration to God's good graces through Christ in the Church. Insisting that virginity is not merely the highest, but the core of all virtue, Methodius concedes that this fact has not been made known to mankind from the beginning.

[24]SC 95, 52.
[25]SC 95, 106-108.

It was not given to the first generations. For in those days there were but few human beings. Hence, it was necessary that their numbers be first increased and brought to viability. Thus, it was no disgrace for ancient men to marry their own sisters. It was only when the Law came that it forbade and denounced as sinful what had previously been considered virtuous. It then placed a curse on whoever would uncover the nakedness of his own sister. *Symposium* 1.2[26]

Methodius next discusses God's method of dealing with mankind. He reflects the teaching of both Irenaeus and Clement of Alexandria regarding God and Christ as the divine pedagogue.

God in his goodness assisted the human race with proper gradualness as do fathers in dealing with their offspring. For they do not hand their infants over to pedagogues immediately, but let them run about in their early years like frisky lambs. Then they entrust them to teachers to guide them through their stammerings until the shackles of their minds are loosened and they are ready for more serious activities.

In this way we believe God has acted with our forefathers. For the world was underpopulated in its infancy. It had to be led from this situation and grow to mature adulthood ... When the world became populous, overflowing with countless numbers from end to end ... they were to advance from brother-sister relations to marriage with women from other families ... The next step was to take them from adultery and advance them on to continence. From continence they come to virginity in which they train themselves to make little of the flesh and anchor themselves firmly in the haven of immortality. *Symposium* 1.2[27]

[26]SC 95, 56-58.
[27]SC 95, 58.

Faced with the objection that the prophets of the Old Testament seemed almost unaware of the spiritual value of virginity, Methodius countered that the revelation of the supremacy of this state of life was reserved for announcement by the Savior. It was his privilege to reveal the good news of this great truth. He would himself provide an example by living as the Archvirgin. Employing the distinction between mankind's creation in God's image and his obligation to achieve the likeness of God by his virtuous strivings, Methodius explains the Christian approach to what the pagans and Plato had taught as divinization—gradually becoming like to God by a virtuous life.

> It was precisely this that the Word was to accomplish by coming into the world. He took upon himself our human form, tarnished and stained as it is by our many sins, in order that we should receive in turn the divine form which he bore for our sake. Thus, it became possible for us to truly fashion ourselves in God's likeness. *Symposium* 1, 4[28]

Replying to an observation of Marcella, Methodius has the second symposiast, Theophila, observe that while mankind had made slow and gradual progress towards chastity, God had no intention of ruling out the process of procreation despite its incompatibility with virginity.

> I think I perceive clearly in the Scriptures the fact that God did not abolish procreation with the coming of virginity *via* the Word. The light of the stars is not extinguished because the moon is larger ... God's ordinance and declaration in *Genesis* is still being observed in regard to begetting children. The Creator is still fashioning people. God, like an artist, is still working on his universe ... thus, man must cooperate in the production of God's image as long as the universe exists ... *Symposium* 2.1[29]

[28]SC 96, 62-64.
[29]SC 96, 68.

The narrator them embarks on a frank description of the physical nature of procreation.

> Man's coming into being begins with the sowing of seed in the furrows of the maternal field. Thus, 'bone from bone' and 'flesh from flesh' are combined through an invisible cooperation of power by the divine craftsman and a new human being is formed. *Ibid.*[30]

Citing the *Genesis* myth of Eve's creation from Adam's rib during his divinely induced sleep, the narrator continues:

> Perhaps the symbolism of that ecstatic sleep into which God cast the first man was meant to typify man's enchantment with love when in his desire for children he falls into a trance lulled by the pleasures of procreation ... Under the stimulus of intercourse the body's harmony—so we are told by those who have experienced the intimacies of marriage—is greatly disturbed. All the marrow-like generative part of the blood that is liquid bone, gathers from all parts of the body and, curdled and worked into foam, rushes through the generative organs into the living soil of the woman. Thus, it is rightly said that 'a man shall leave father and mother' to be as one flesh in the embrace of life ... *Symposium* 1, 2, 2[31]

There is no trace of a puritanic approach to sex in this consideration; nor, when introducing the problem of children illegally begotten through adultery, is there any attempt to evade reality.

Emphasizing the pertinence of this observation, the narrator continued:

> Very many people who have been born out of wedlock are, notwithstanding, not only thought worthy of being admitted among the flock of our brethren; they are even

[30]SC 96, 70.
[31]SC 95, 70.

often chosen for position or authority. Since it is clear that those conceived adulterously are allowed to develop to maturity ... *Discourse* 3, 2[32]

Methodius denies that the practice of chastity consists in the repression of sexual desires to the neglect of other virtues.

Neither does he who loves himself excessively and strives always to look to his own private good regardless of his neighbor, do honor to chastity ... Indeed he dishonors it. For he is far from the number of those who worthily cultivate this virtue. No it is not proper to practice chastity and virginity and then become defiled and incontinent by evil deeds; or to profess purity and self-control and then become polluted by sin; or to say that we are not concerned with the things of this world, and then try to possess them and make ourselves anxious over them. Rather all our members must be preserved intact and untouched by corruption, not only the actual organs of generation but all other that stimulate them. Thus, it would be ridiculous to keep one's generative organs pure but not one's tongue; or to keep one's tongue pure but not one's sight, one's ears or hands; or to keep all these pure, but not one's heart, allowing it to consort with anger and conceit. *Symposium* 11[33]

Methodius sees the actuality of mankind's redemption in terms of the fall in Adam and in Christ's assumption of the status of the first man to redeem the human race from sinfulness and perdition. But he again feels the necessity of contending with the long trajectory of mankind's history before the intervention of Christ.

After the fall, man wanted to be under the rule of virtue once more and not excluded from the pleasures of

[32]SC 95, 74.
[33]SC 95, 306.

immortality of Paradise. But having sinned he was rejected and cast out being no longer capable of sustaining immortality.

The first message of mankind after the fall came through Noah by which mankind might have been saved from sin had they listened ... It promised joy and a cessation of troubles if they would observe the message according to man's abilities ... But this precept, no matter how zealously preached by Noah, mankind could not obey ...

And so when those people were rejected by divine providence, and the human race once more given over to error, God sent them a new Law through Moses to govern and recall them to the path of righteousness. This, too, they forgot and returned to idol worship. So God gave them up to mutual slaughter, exile and captivity ... The Law itself refused to attempt to save them ... Then God took pity and a fourth time sent them chastity ... This brought great benefit and assistance to mankind since it was the only precept the devil was not able to counterfeit for the deception of mankind. *Symposium* 10.3[34]

Continuing his analogy:

It was for this reason that the Word assumed human nature that by himself he might defeat the serpent and annul the condemnation that existed for man's ruin. It was truly fitting that the Evil One should be defeated by no other than the one the devil boasted he had ruled since he first deceived him ... Just as in Adam all men die, so also in Christ who assumed Adam, all were made to come alive.

[34]SC 95, 292-94.

While he fails to approach the metaphysical problem involved in the existence of evil, Methodius does tackle the concern with free will that was so much a part of the philosophical milieu of his day.

> Those who maintain that man has not free will but is governed by the inevitable necessities and the unwritten decrees of fate commit impiety against God himself.
>
> For they, thus, declare that he is the source and cause of man's sins. For if he directs the entire circles of the stars in harmonious motion with his mysterious and inscrutable wisdom and the stars produce the qualities of vice and virtue in life, thus, impelling men to these things by the bonds of necessity, they proclaim God as the source and origin of evil ... *Symposium* 8, 16[35]

Confronting the popular philosophies of the day, Methodius maintains:

> Those who truly know Christ do not remain constantly as children. They are not like the Greeks who hide the truth in myth and fiction rather than deal with it in a rational fashion ... According to them, the Zodiac is made up of a number of figures called the Twelve Signs going from Aries to Pisces and their make-up is based upon mythological events ... *Discourse* 8, 15[36]
>
> Of all the evils implanted among us, the worst is to attribute the origin of sin to the influence of the stars and the doctrine that our lives are controlled by the impulses of fate ... *Discourse* 8, 16[37]

[35]SC 95, 248.
[36]SC 95, 240.
[37]SC 95, 248.

Methodius is a witness to the gradually maturing concepts of the Christian moral perspective. His writings had a
definite influence on the development of the Church's self-
consciousness and help us to better comprehend the daily
life of the well-educated Christian of the early fourth
century.

Chapter Four

The West: Carthage and Rome

Tertullian

Under the aegis of *legisperiti* or law-oriented converts to the Christian religion, the ethical consciousness of the western Church took its rise. The two foremost figures were the brash, abrasive and thoroughly learned Tertullian and the more humane but equally effective Cyprian of Carthage. Of Tertullian's lineage and status in the Church we know nothing other than that he was a successful lawyer and married man with both a Hellenic and Roman education. He seems to have been attracted to Christianity at first by the steadfastness of the martyrs.

Of Cyprian, we know that he was a well-known orator and advocate whose conversion was due to his disenchantment with the secular society of his day. His acceptance of the Christian faith and subsequent selection as a priest and bishop evidently stirred concern in the local Carthaginian community, occasioning several of his writings as personal apologetics. Tertullian's apologetic on the other hand is objective in scope, answering the calumnies and charges of ill-faith and treason levelled against the Christians.

In the development of the western theology, a legalistic savor prevails. Men like Lactantius, Hilary of Poitiers and Ambrose of Milan give evidence of an orientation centered on the Law of God, interpreting the biblical 'Law and the Prophets' with the assistance of a rhetorician's, if not a jurisprudential awareness. This is not quite characteristic of the Roman ecclesiastics, the more biblically oriented churchmen, such as Jerome, Rufinus and, above all, Augustine. But the imprint of Tertullian's absolutistic preoccupation with the divine will as the source of human obligation and the legal terminology in which he expressed his theological thinking prevailed in the western Church down to modern times.

It is unfortunate that we do not possess detailed information concerning Tertullian's conversion to Christianity. For he is the first, outstanding, western theologian. As such, his doctrinal formation as well as the breadth of his moral interests are remarkable. In his earliest writings, he demonstrates a fully supernatural awareness as well as a ready familiarity with both the Old and the New Testament. He is well informed concerning the Church's tradition and early history. Despite his subsequent defection into the heresy of Montanism, he possessed a solid grasp of Catholic doctrine which he expresses in his numerous writings with vigor, and frequently with a brilliance verging on the bizarre. Not strictly an original thinker, Tertullian is dependent on his predecessors, the Apologists of the second century, for the substance of his thought. An incomparable stylist, however, he gives classic expression to many of the fundamental notions of Christian teaching. In the moral sphere, likewise, his opinions betray originality only when they run to extremes. But he is witness to a vivid moral awareness that goes to the very heart of the Christian way of life.

In his preoccupation with the faith in all its aspects, Tertullian introduces into the theology of the West a whole diapason of legal concepts and terms that perdure in the Latin Church down to the present. He opts for the Law of

Christ, but his explanation of that Law takes on many features of the Roman legal system in words, concepts, figures of speech, similitudes and arguments, many of which greatly influence the western Church's explanation of the Incarnation, the Redemption and the Christian way of life. Thus, for Tertullian, God is the legislator, a judge administering the law. Justice is that which pervades the relations between God and man. The Gospel is our law, and sin consists of breaking the law. By a fault, the guilty offend God; hence, amends must be made by way of satisfaction. Where Irenaeus spoke of salvation under the aspect of the divine economy, Tertullian talks of the salutary discipline of God's Law.

A brilliant lawyer who had apparently achieved considerable sucess in Roman legal spheres, Tertullian's earliest interest in Christianity seems to have been elicited by the steadfastness of the martyrs. Thence his attention was attracted to the sublimity and coherence of the Christian moral teaching. Fr. Adhémar d'Alès in his classic elucidation of Tertullian's theology, *La Théologie de Tertullien,* Paris, 1905, has several excellent pages on his subject's appreciation of the historical development of the divine law as it appears in the course of God's revelation, and as it is depicted in the Sacred Scriptures. (See especially Chapter Six).

Tertullian sees the substance of the Divine Law expressed seminally in the original command given to Adam in the garden of Eden. The prohibition to eat of the forbidden fruit thus contained in germ all the precepts of the decalog. The patriarchs, instructed by nature - *naturaliter* - came to recognize and practice the essential commandments which had been engraved in their hearts.

> Before the Law of Moses ... there was a Law, I maintain, not written which was naturally known and observed by our forefathers ... As became God's goodness and equity, as the maker of the human race, he gave the same

Law to all peoples. And that which he commanded was to
be observed in certain prescribed times when he wished,
as he wished it, and by those whom he wished. *Against
the Jews II* 7[1]

Tertullian thus manifests a consciousness of the various
stages of the Law as it was given to mankind in different
circumstances.

In the beginning of the world he gave a law to Adam and
Eve that they should not eat of the fruit of the tree planted
in the midst of the garden of paradise; if they did, they
would die the death (Genesis 2:7). This law would have
sufficed if they had kept it. For in that law given to Adam
we recognize the basis for all the commandments that
afterward were to reverberate in those given through
Moses ... *Ibid. II* 2-3[2]

Because they conformed their conduct to the divine will,
Noah, Abraham, Melchisedech and Henoch among others,
were saints; hence friends of Almighty God. Moses gave
mankind a written law which was, however, provisional.
For, as explained by the prophets, God intended it as a
direct preparation for the new and definitive dispensation
that would be inaugurated with the coming of Christ. With
the preaching of the Gospel, Christ decreed the abolition of
circumcision and the ritualistic observance of the Sabbath,
and of the ancient sacrifices. He inaugurated a new rule of
the Spirit. However, the Gospels in fact re-promulgated and
perfected the precepts of the natural law.

The primordial law given to Adam and Eve in paradise
was, as it were, the matrix of all God's precepts. Since, if
they had loved the Lord their God, they would not have
gone against his command. If they loved their neighbor,

[1]CCL, 2, 1342.
[2]CCL 2, 1341.

that is one another, they would not have given in to the persuasion of the serpent; and they would not have committed homicide on each other by cutting themselves off from immortality. *Ibid.*

Parallel with an appreciation of the gradual revelation of God's law in the course of human history, Tertullian elucidates a theory of human responsibility that is both realistic and orthodox in the strictest connotation of those terms. He sees man as an individual composite of soul and body, answerable before God for the activities of each of his faculties, both spiritual and physical. Man is created by God in his own image - hence he is endowed with reason and free will. Unfortunately, however, man can employ his freedom to offend God, misusing either or both soul and body for evil purposes. Associated in life until sundered in the final moment of death, these two elements of the human being will be joined together in the resurrrection for the reward or punishment to which man's deeds entitle him. Together they will undergo the same judgment before God who sees into the utmost recesses of the human heart, and whose justice is inexorable.

I find man created by God having free will and self control, no more conscious of the image and likeness of God in him than the form of his status. For it is not in his face and bodily line that are so varied in the human race that he is made in God's form, but in that substance that he draws from God, that is his soul. The latter responds to the form of God and is co-signed with liberty and self-possession. And this status, the law itself confirms ... for a law would not be prescribed for one who did not have the proper obedience in his power, nor would there be the threat of death for a transgression if contempt for the law and freedom of the will had not been extended to man ... *Against Marcion 2, 5; 5-7*[3]

[3]CCL 1, 480.

Tertullian finds the root of man's ability to do evil in the will. Making proper allowance for human actions that happen by inadvertence or accident, he traces man's conscious acts to the responsibility of his free will. Difficulties, no matter what their magnitude, do not destroy the will's freedom, hence they cannot justify man's conduct when he chooses to do evil. The perfection of the law introduced by Christ consists precisely in the reprobation of sins committed interiorly with the will. To enjoy in the mind the contemplation of a sinful deed is already to be guilty of sin. Thus Christ classed lustful desire as the equivalent of adultery. He made hatred the equivalent of murder.

> But what of free will as the cause of our action? We can certainly eliminate the sins that happen by accident, necessity or ignorance. Outside of those, however, there is no sin except in the will ... Finally how does the Lord add to the law other than by forbidding sins of the will? For he describes as an adulterer not only the person who violates the marriage of another by conjugal relations, but the man who befouls it by a lustful look. *On Penitence* 3, 11-14[4]

Tertullian further insists that man's conscience is immediately burdened with the necessity of interpreting God's law correctly; and for this purpose the Christian is endowed with grace. But he maintains,

> There is no excusing cause which saves men from punishment even when they know not the Lord - for ignorance of God is not excusable, since He is set plainly before men and can be known through the very gifts we have received from heaven - how much more perilous it is to despise Him who, having received from Him a knowledge of good and evil, insults his own understanding, which is

[4]CCL 2, 325.

God's gift, by taking up again what he knows he should forswear and what he has already forsworn. *On Penitence* 5, 4-5[5]

In a brilliant bit of satire, Tertullian rules out all equivocation in the moral order:

> Some say, however, that God is satisfied if He be honored in heart and mind, even though this be not done externally. Thus they sin, yet lose not reverential fear and faith. That is to say, they lose not chastity and commit adultery! They lose not filial piety and poison a parent! So also will they not lose pardon and be cast down into hell, seeing that they sin and lose not reverential fear. A wonderful example of wrongheadedness: because they fear, they sin! I suppose they would not sin if they did not fear. On this principle, he who does not wish God to be offended should have no reverence for Him at all, if it is fear that sponsors his offense. *Ibid.* 10-13[6]

Together with having a clear concept of original sin, Tertullian stresses the necessity of repentance for sin, as well as participation in the redemption through Baptism and the continual imitation of Christ by a life of mortification, almsgiving and prayer. In his Catholic period, likewise, he testifies clearly to the discipline of penance in the Church, even though there is still considerable uncertainty as to the particulars of that practice.

Two further considerations serve to clarify Tertullian's theorizing with regard to the foundations of man's moral obligations. They enable us to see somewhat more clearly the genesis of this late, second-century moralist's rigoristic tendencies. In his *Against Marcion*, Tertullian takes up the problem of evil in its generic or philosophical aspect. This was a matter that greatly concerned his contemporaries. It

[5]CCL 2, 328.
[6]CCL 2, 329.

was evidently, likewise, a topic met with frequently in the apocryphal writings both of the late Jewish and the early Christian milieu.

In his solution of the problem of evil, then, Tertullian reflects orthodox Christian belief. But he so stresses the power of the evil spirits in the world as to arrive at a state of mind wherein he gradually comes to repudiate the distinctions he had earlier acknowledged between God's precepts and the counsels. He had conceded that while desiring man's achievement of perfection in all his doings, God in his mercy made allowance for human weakness, tolerating man's accomplishment of lesser goods. Turned Montanist, he gradually retracted the neat distinctions he had arrived at in his earlier writings. He comes to interpret the counsels as positive commands.

In justifying the goodness of God - as projected in his creation of man - Tertullian proceeds to demonstrate the supreme reasonableness of God's having fashioned man after His own image and likeness. Having endowed man with reason and free will, he says, God had likewise to give him control over his actions and desires, that man might demonstrate his interior goodness. For God alone is good by nature. Man was created as a physically good thing; but he had to achieve spiritual goodness in order that he might worthily receive the reward God set before him. The fact that God does not prevent man from doing the evil which God foresees him doing is not an argument against either God's goodness or His power. Rather does it attest to His reasonability and His justice. For he has delivered a Law to man which is not intended to destroy his liberty, but rather to assist him in achieving the goodness for which he was created. God created man for eternal life. It is man's evil doings that introduced the necessity of death.

> Freedom of the will does not refer its wrongdoing to him by whom it was given, but to him who used it as he should not have. How then can you ascribe Evil to the Creator, if the fault is man's, not God's; nor is the same to be considered the author of the wrongdoing who is the

interdictor, indeed the one to condemn. If death is an evil, death is not to be ascribed to the one who threatened it but to the one who commanded it as its author. *Against Marcion* 2.9, 9[7]

Hence the fault is not be attributed to God that man freely misused the gift of free will. For man had been endowed with greater power than the evil angel who seduced him into committing sin. In Tertullian's thought, man, as the image of God, is by nature greater than the "material spirit" of which the angels are created.

It is at this point in his argument that we get a glimpse of the reasoning that Tertullian employs to justify himself in his decided rigorism. For he maintains that, before the Fall, God had dealt with man in the most generous fashion. It is only as a result of man's sin that God becomes a severe judge.

> Now, woman is condemned to bring forth children in sorrow, and to serve man; but before, without trace of sadness she had heard of the increment with a blessing: *"Increase and multiply!"* and this was to be accomplished in cooperation with man, not in servitude to him ... Now, there is sweat and labor for bread; before, of every tree, there was unlabored food and secure nourishment ... *Against Marcion* 2, 11[8]

Thus God's goodness in accordance with His nature was first demonstrated to man; now He has been forced to show man His severity.

There is a further consideration in keeping with this development, that becomes increasingly clear as we trace Tertullian's application of his moral doctrines to the activities of everyday life. It is his pre-occupation with the presence and power of the devil in the world. His treatise *On Idolatry* (written ca. 208-212) has for its thesis the fact that

[7]CCL 2, 486.
[8]CCL 2, 488.

the evil spirits, while inhabiting the air, are behind all pagan, secular activity. Hence Tertullian feels the necessity of reminding the Christian of his promise made in Baptism to reject the devil with his "works and pomps". He indicates the innumerable situations in which the Christian cannot join his pagan neighbors without perjuring himself as a Christian in consequence of his original promise to repudiate the *pompa diaboli*.

With vivid imagination and uncompromising logic, Tertullian proceeds to elaborate a theme that was fairly common in the theological literature of the day. In the Jewish apocryphal book of *Henoch*, the statement is made that the fallen angels let themselves be seduced by the daughters of man. Josephus and Philo, Irenaeus and some of the Apologists, as well as the earlier Alexandrian Fathers repeat this legend. For Tertullian it becomes a crucial proof of the demoniac presence in the world.

In view of his belief that angels had at least a partially material nature, this theory is not as absurd on Tertullian's part as it would be, had he a clearer idea of the angels as pure spirits. In any case, Tertullian believes that from this union were born new series of demons more perverse than the original fallen angels. Like the latter, however, they are engaged in luring man to spiritual destruction. In particular, they are attempting to avenge themselves on Almighty God by perverting his favored creature, man, to whom salvation has been offered in Baptism. For there is no redemption for the devil and his demons.

To these evil spirits Tertullian attributes in particular the revelation to man of various arts - from the methods for using metals and employing herbs as medicines, to the perversity of incantation and the interpretation of the stars. In a special way they have turned against womankind, using her sex for the furthering of their evil wiles. They have taught her the devices of vanity; they have coached her in the artifices to be used in seducing man through improving her appearance with cosmetics and the adornments of precious stones and jewelry.

But the theme truly characteristic of Tertullian's conviction is his conclusion that the entire public life of the pagan city was interpenetrated by demoniac influences. This is the burden of his monograph *On the Spectacles*. Not alone are the pagan and other false religions in reality the cult of the devil, but the public squares, the forum, the baths, the theatres, even the very homes of the pagans are all dedicated to idols. Hence they are the property of the demons.

> "Satan and his angels are in possession of this whole world," he says, while acknowledging that "the world is of God, but worldliness is of the devil." *On Spectacles* 8, 9[9]

Tertullian joins to this assertion the further consideration that since man's evil propensities are demoniacally inspired, it is but normal that attendance at public spectacles can but expose the Christian to the stimulation of his evil passions. His satire is eloquent, his sarcasm and irony reach new depths of bitterness as he describes the stimulation to violence, to cruelty, and sensuality, to the service of mammon, that accompanies attendance at public functions.

What renders the final appreciation of the moral thought of Tertullian doubly difficult is the paucity of information we possess concerning the organization of the Church in Carthage at the turn of the third century. We are uncertain as to his true status as cleric or priest. Nor do we have any true knowledge of his adversaries. The circumstances surrounding his defection from the Catholic Church are badly in need of clarification. What is clear is that he does accept the revelations of the Montanist apostles concerning the newly inaugurated reign of the Holy Spirit. But he registers few of the truly extravagant claims or excesses with which this heresy is associated. His interest seems to be rather a rebellion against the moral mediocrity of the Catholics whom he satirically refers to as the *Psychics*. He goads and

[9]CCL 1, 235.

lashes at his former co-religionists for their failure to take a much stricter and, therefore, more spiritual attitude towards sin, imperfection, and the things of this world. This is particularly evident in the complicated evidence he provides in his *De Paenitentia* - written while still a Catholic - and in his *De Pudicitia*, concerning the remission of sins. Even when he speaks of "irremissible sins," his polemic is directed against the Church. He admits that God can and does forgive apostasy, murder and adultery. In his heretical period, when writing about mainly dogmatic subjects, such as in his *On the Resurrection of the Body* and *On the Flesh of Christ*, he remains within orthodox lines.

What preserves Tertullian from the charge of having been an authentic Puritan or Jansenist before-the-fact, is the candor with which he acknowledges his own sexual deliquencies before conversion, without in the least exaggerating or exhibiting an obsessional concern of fear or guilt in this regard. Likewise, the extreme frankness with which he writes of sex, both in his technical treatises such as the *de Anima*, and in his numerous flayings of debauchery and excess, reveal a mature and even a healthy attitude towards these matters. He is unmerciful in the savagery he exhibits towards the perpetrators of immorality, mordently ironic in taxing the *Psychics* with a mediocre spirituality. But he is neither morbid, nor in the strict sense, an exhibitionist, for all that he is is an overbearing egotist.

The foundation of Tertullian's moral teaching, then, is provided by a clear and integrated appreciation of the law of God as revealed to man in the several stages of sacred history. On a background of a valid anthropology, Tertullian elaborates the application of the Ten Commandments as they are promulgated anew in the Christian dispensation. He sees the baptized Christian living under a supernatural order, whose destiny in eternity is jeopardized by man's propensity to give in to the temptations of a legion of demons. In his Catholic period, though severe in his moral judgments, he is just an orthodox. Turned Montanist, he seems to feel that the Church is unwilling to face up to the actuality of the reign of the Spirit; that despite the teaching

of Christ, St. Paul, and the twelfth chapter of the Apoca-
lypse, it was not sufficiently conscious of the demoniac
power in the world. Hence in the application of the exigencies of God's moral law, he tends to run to an extreme
rigorism. But in the end he justifies himself by insisting that
as man is made in the image of his creator, the spiritual part
of his being is so much superior to the material or physical
that it is ridiculous to think that he cannot, with God's
grace, assert the predominance of the spiritual over the
material.

> But we read that the flesh is weak, and we acknowledge
> this in certain people. But we also learn that the spirit is
> strong. For in one sense both are posed. The flesh is
> worldly material, the spirit celestial. Why then are we
> more prone to excuse ourselves pointing out the things
> that are weak rather than taking stock of the strong? Why
> do not worldly things cede before celestial?[10]

Almost forgotten in the Middle Ages due to the dispar-
agement of the Decree of Gelasius, Tertullian comes into
prominence with the Renaissance. Attempts innumerable
have been made to fathom the personality of Tertullian, to
describe his genius, and probe the qualities of his mind.
With the advent of modern psychology and the techniques
of psychoanalysis, it is strange that much more attention
has not been given to this aggressive, egotistical, and certainly overpowering personality. B. Nisters devoted a modest effort to describing the character of Tertullian in terms of
Kretschmer's psychological typing. What is revealing is the
fact that Nisters concludes that Tertullian was not a psycho-
path in any true sense of that term, although he gives every
indication of characteristics beyond what is conceded generally as normal. Particularly in dealing with Tertullian's
attitude toward sex, Nisters has preserved an eminently
common sense as well as scientific attitude. It is in this realm

[10]CCL 1, 377.

that one would expect rather startling conclusions. The extreme lengths to which Tertullian goes in his descriptions of the foibles of women, the savage if exquisite satire, and the mordant wit he employs in accusing the pagans of debauchery and perversion, and the bitterness in which, after his Montanist defection, he ascribes sensuality to the Catholics, would all seem to provide lurid material for the psychiatrist. In fact, however, Nisters places this evidence in its proper literary and stylistic perspective. Tertullian is but improving on a long-standing fashion among the pagan moralists. To his rigorism in matters of sex, likewise, Nisters ascribes an, at least, seemingly legitimate objective: the creation of a Christian elite who would accept the full implication of the Gospel and Pauline doctrine concering chastity and virginity, and who would thereby justify his claim that chastity was the foundation of sanctity. Tertullian's gradual hardening in the campaign against second marriages was a result of the Montanist movement in which that issue seems to have become a "battle cry."

Together with a bizarre imagination, an excellent memory, an extravagant vocabulary, and a startling literary style, Tertullian was possessed of a supremely quick, logical mind. He could hurtle through, from premise to a third- or fourth-removed conclusion with the brilliance of a bolt of lightning. But in so doing, he frequently ignored circumstances that altered the nature of the intermediate premises, thus invalidating his logical conclusion.

Cyprian of Carthage

Well within the theological tradition set by Tertullian, but of a totally different temperament, Caecilius Thasius Cyprian was both a famous rhetorician turned Christian and a bishop of Carthage selected by the community in ca. 249, a few years after his conversion and ordination to the priesthood. Of his episcopal career his writings supply a vivid account, not the least of which was his flight to safe-keeping at the outbreak of the Decian persecution in AD

250 with his pagan fellow-citizens shouting, "Cyprian to the lions!" Both his selection as bishop after so short an introduction to Christianity and his flight occasioned controversy. In a letter to the priests of Rome, who challenged his conduct, he wrote:

> I believe it proper to send you this letter ... by way of clarifying my activities, my discipline and my diligence. As the Lord's prediction advises, at the first outbreak of the upheaval, when the populace began to call for me repeatedly with violence, I decided to withdraw for the moment. I was concerned not so much with my own safety as with the well-being of our faithful. For my presence seemed to be adding further provocation to the tumult that had broken out. While absent in body, I was not lacking in spirit or in action or in advice and did not fail my brethren by a lack of counsel. *Letter 20*[11]

With this letter Cyprian enclosed thirteen others detailing his pastoral concerns and activities in Carthage as a result of the persecution. His writings are dictated by his evangelical commitments. They include a tract written for a friend, Donatus, giving an account of his conversion. He likewise wrote a rebuttal of anti-Christian accusations in a tract on *Mortality* to Demetrius. Inspired by Tertullian - in his *On Illustrious Men*, Jerome tells us that Cyprian called for Tertullian's works with the command, *Da mihi magristrum* (hand me the master) - he produced a number of tracts including *On the Lapsed, On the Clothing of Virgins, On the Unity of the Church, On Patience, On Good Works and Almsgiving, On Prayer*, and *On Martyrdom*.

In his account of his conversion, addressed to Donatus, he asserts:

> Caught in a web of darkness and blinding night and bound by the chains of a boastful world, fluctuating

[11]CSEL 3, 2, 527, cf ACW 43, 101

between doubt and aberration, unconscious of my true life, alien to truth and enlightenment, I began with great difficulty to consider those moral values that by divine indulgence promised me salvation - viz. that one could be reborn by a washing in the water of salvation into a new way of life, and one could put off what he had been formerly, and yet retain the integrity of the body while changing in mind and spirit. *To Donatus* 1[12]

Cyprian goes on to detail the contents of this change:

Thus I was thinking to myself. And I was conscious of being inplicated in so many errors during my past life out of which I did not believe I could extricate myself. I was thus involved in the vices surrounding me and I was in despair of better things since I favored my evil doings as my possessions and servants. But as Light was poured into me through the engendering wave (of Baptism) and the stain of my former life was washed away, I felt my inner-being now cleansed and pure. And after a new birth had reconstructed me as a new man through the heavenly Spirit, my doubts were suddenly calmed in a wonderful manner. As hidden things became clear to me, and the darkness lifted, I received the ability to do what previously seemed so difficult... and I began to feel that what the Holy Spirit had animated in me was of God. *To Donatus 1*[12]

Cyprian was not a professional theologian. But he was a meditative man of action who gave a clear account of his stewardship in caring for his not unsophisticated flock. In his writings he felt compelled to supply a reasoned justification for his manifold decisions in the moral and spiritual realm. By way of a background to his thinking, he made a collection of the Gospel injunctions concerning the moral life under some 120 headings and published this scriptural catch-all as *Testimonies*. It was not a unique literary form

[12]CCL 111A. 10

and would be duplicated a century later by Basil of Caesarea; but it gave an evangelical savor to his proclamation of the Law of Christ.

In his *On the Lord's Prayer* Cyprian insists:

> The precepts of the Gospel are nothing other than divine teaching, the foundation of a budding hope, the basis for a strengthening of the faith, the directional guide-posts on a highway, and the foundations of the way of salvation. They thus provide instruction for the minds of believers who are docile during their earthly career and lead to the heavenly kingdom.[13]

In his *On Good Works and Almsgiving*, Cyprian supplies a theological background for understanding man and the fall.

> 1. For when the Lord came to heal the wounds that Adam bore, and to disinfect the ancient poisons of the serpent, he gave a law to the one he healed. He then prescribed that mankind sin no more, lest something worse befall the sinner. We were thus constrained and shepherded in a narrow path of innocence by his command. Nor could we have had what even only human weakness and infirmity could achieve unless the divine mercy intervened. 2. By pointing out the works of justice and mercy, (God) opened a path leading to salvation, so that we could cancel out our evil doing by almsgiving. Those of you who are rich therefore, buy yourselves the fire-tested gold of Christ. Sloughing off your evils, you may be pure and clean, purged through your alms and works of justice.[14]

[13]CCL 111A. 90
[14]CCL 11A. 55, 56, 63

Cyprian's was a social view of the Church. He insists:

> Before all, (Christ) the doctor of peace and the teacher of
> unity did not want our prayer to be individual and pri-
> vate. Thus when someone prays, it is not for the self
> alone. For we do not say "My father who is in heaven,"
> nor "Give me today my daily bread." Nor does anyone
> ask to have his own sins alone forgiven, nor request to be
> liberated from evil and temptation for oneself alone ...
> Our prayer is a public and communal prayer. *On the
> Lord's Prayer* 8[15]

Nevertheless, he insists that prayer be fervent and atten-
tive, describing with realism the distractions that beset one
while praying:

> Your heart should be closed to the enemy (Satan) and
> open to God alone. Nor should the adversary of God be
> allowed to be present in time of prayer. For he frequently
> pesters and subtly penetrates to distract our prayers from
> God so that we have one thing in our voice but another in
> our heart when we owe God sincere attention and should
> pray, not in the sound of the voice, but with mind and
> consciousness. What a foolishness it is to be alienated and
> taken up with inept and profane thoughts when calling on
> the Lord, as if there were anything greater about which to
> think than that you are talking to God. *On the Lord's
> Prayer* 31[16]

Cyprian explains God's providence in dealing with sinfulness:

> We acknowledge the salutary gift of divine indulgence. It
> amends and purges our sins since we cannot exist without
> some wound in our conscience. It allows us to cure these
> wounds with spiritual remedies... Nor let anyone boast
> of a pure and immaculate heart... Since no one can be
> without sin, if someone says he is without fault, he is

[15]CSEL 3, 1, 271.
[16]CSEL 3, 289.

either proud or stupid.... Yet how necessary and benign is the divine mercy. It knows that, even after the cure, there will not be lacking certain wounds, and has given us salutary remedies for curing and healing our infirmities. *On Good Works and Almsgiving*, 3[17]

Dealing with the problems brought on the Church of Carthage following the persecutions, Cyprian attempted to follow a benevolent policy in judging those who had betrayed the faith out of fear of losing their possessions or in the course of actual torture. He constructs a realistic picture of one of the lapsed:

I had indeed desired to fight courageously; and mindful of my sacramental vow, I took with me the arms of faith and devotion. But in the course of the torment and beatings, I was overcome. My intention remained stable and my faith strong, and my mind fought long in these torments... But when the rising savagery of the hardhearted judge ordered me already exhausted to be flogged and my nails pulled out, and flames applied, my flesh deserted me in the battle, and the infirmity of my reins ceded. Not the soul, but the body gave in with sorrow. *On the Lapsed* 13[18]

Such a case, Cyprian concedes, can quickly be given forgiveness and the miserable Christian excused. But the bishop's task was not that simple. For so-called Confessors of the Faith, Christians who had not yielded to the torturer's demands and who had survived, now considered themselves chosen by God to show mercy to the lapsed, granting them a share in their sufferings, and thus a pardon for the sins of their weakness. The pride and arrogance of many of these "Confessors" was disturbing the faithful. Hence, Cyprian found himself forced to insist that forgiveness of sin required both sorrow and serious penitential practices.

[17]CSEL 3, 1, 375.
[18]CSEL 3, 1, 246.

He complains bitterly of the activity of the so-called "Confessors" who granted pardons or indulgences to the lapsed Catholics without demanding penance:

> All these remedies being neglected, before their sins are expiated, before *exhomologesis* — the program of forgiveness through intense penitence — has been made for the crime, and before their conscience has been purged by sacrifice and the hand of the priest...they now inflict more of a crime by mouth and hand against the Lord than when they actually renounced Him. Let no one deceive himself...Only the Lord can show mercy...Man cannot forgive sin or grant an indulgence for a crime committed against the Lord...In the Gospel, the Lord spoke as follows: Who confesses me before the Father...but who denies me...If he does not repudiate the one denying him, neither will the Lord...*On the Lapsed* 16[19]

In dealing with the everyday problems of the Christian in the world, Cyprian took a definitely adverse attitude toward the theater and public spectacles. Confronted with the problem of a converted actor who plead poverty in not abandoning his profession, Cyprian wrote:

> I do not think that this is in keeping with either the divine majesty nor evangelical discipline that the honor and decency of the church should be dirtied with such vile and infamous contagion.

> Nor is anyone excused if refraining from the theater itself he still teaches this to others. He is not perceived to have deserted who substitutes other things and suggests in his place many others against the institution of God, teaching and coaching how a male acts as a woman and changes sex by skill; rather he pleases the devil by sullying divine flesh through the sins of a corrupt and enervated body.

[19]CSEL 3, 1, 248.

And if such a one proposes his penury and the necessity of proverty, he can along with the others who are supported by the elements of the Church be assisted in these necessities if only he will be content with more frugal and innocent foods. Nor should he think he should be rewarded with a salary for having ceased from sin, since this is not for his own good. *Epistle* 2[20].

Cyprian had to deal likewise with a more delicate difficulty.

On virgins who maintan their status firmly and continently, but at the same time had been detected living with men .. and those who confess that they sleep with men yet assert that they are still intact .. In the first place we do not allow our faithful to err, but we faithfully counsel them not to cohabit with men. I am not saying to sleep together but not to even live together since their sex is weak and their still lubricious age should be restrained and in all things ruled by us. If they do not want to persevere or cannot, it is better that they marry than fall into the fire for their sins.

Hence lest the undisciplined are consumed and perish, do as far as you can to regulate the fraternity with wholesome counsels. Narrow and difficult is the way by which we enter into life. Who castrate themselves for the kingdom of heaven fully please God and let not the priests of God offend the Church by the scandal of their evil doing. And if they obey us, we have gained brothers... If some do not wish to obey, let us follow the Apostle, "If I were to please men, I cannot be Christ's servant."

Nor let anyone think she can defend herself by this excuse that she can be inspected and probed as to whether she is still a virgin.... since both the hand and the eye of the obstetrician often fail. And if the virgin is found uncorrupted in that part of her whereby she is a woman, she can

[20]CSEL 3, 2, 473.

still have sinned in another part of the body that can be corrupted but cannot be seen...If a husband suddenly appears and finds another man lying with his wife, will he not become indignant and sputter and perchance in the sorrow of his anger take sword in hand?

But if they do penance for this illicit sleeping together, and recede among themselves, let these virgins be carefully inspected by the obstetrician and if they are found to be still virgins, let them be welcomed into the Church with this warning that if they return to please some men later they will be punished with graver censure. *Epistle* 6, 1[20]

In response to an inimical pagan critic, Demetrianus, Cyprian composed a tract *On Mortality*. It is a large-scale commentary on the state of the world that lies midway between Tertullian's *Apologeticum* and Augustine's *City of God*.

With you barking against the God who is one and true, Demetrianus, and frequently complaining with a sacrilegious mouth and impious tongue, I could have more reverently and better condemned you by judging the incompetence of your errors and spurning you in silence rather than provoking the insanity of your mindlessness by speaking... For coming at me frequently with the intent of contradicting rather than the desire of learning, and sounding off with clamorous voice, you desire rather to attack impudently than to listen patiently....

The first thing you should realize is that the world has grown old — *senuisse jam seculum* — It is no longer possessed of the strength it once had, nor does the vigor and power of the past still prevail. In the winter there is not that great supply of rain for nourishing the seeds; nor in the summer is there the usual fragrance for ripening the fruits; nor in the spring are there happy temperatures nor in the fall is there fecundity for the trees...

A sentence has been passed on this world. Here the law of God is that all things that rise shall fall; those grown get old, the strong are weakened, great things diminish....

In these last times, evil and adversities multiply and with the day of judgment already approaching the censure of an indignant God on the human race results in more and more plagues. This is not because your gods are not honored by us, but because our God is not worshipped by you. *To Demetrianus On Mortality* 1-7[21]

---

[21]CSEL 3, 1, 351-355.

Chapter Five

The Eastern Fathers

Athanasius of Alexandria

Athanasius, the fourth-century theological polemicist, was condemned as a man of one idea. But that idea was of such significance as to have merited him the sobriquet, Athanasius against the world. His struggle certified the doctrine of the Trinity as the essential Christian belief. It is this Alexandrian churchman who, more than anyone before him, insisted that the Trinity was the foundation of the Christian way of life. In so doing, he used the Greek notion of the *arche* — the first principle, the foundation — to rise above the order of material nature in a search for the origin of man. He found it in the notion of creation. He, thus, literally transcended the heroic Greek effort to achieve a reasonable grasp of the nature of reality that took into account mankind's two-fold nature — the intellectual and the carnal. In reaching beyond the limits of the universe, Athanasius depends totally on divine revelation for his notion of the "first cause uncaused" at which the Greeks in the person of Aristotle had arrived by human wisdom.

Others, among whom is to be numbered Plato ... assert that God made everything out of pre-existing but unfashioned material; and that even God cannot make anything unless matter already pre-existed...thus, they mythologize. But the divine teaching and the faith of Christ reject this inepititude as a detestable impiety ... For things are not made by chance, since they are governed by providence; nor are they made of existing material, but out of nothing through the word as Moses asserts: 'In the beginning God made heaven and earth.'. *On the Incarnation* 2-3.[1]

He concludes:

To think of God as composing and putting the universe together out of matter is a Greek notion. It is to represent Him as a workman (*technites*), not as a Creator (*poiētes*). *On the Incarnation* 2:22[2]

In his *Apologia against the Arians*, Athanasius supplied details of the momentous career he was forced to pursue because of his intransigence in defending the divinity of Christ. As deacon to Bishop Alexander of Alexandria at the Council of Nicea in 325, he was responsible for the use of the word *homoousios* — of the same nature — to clarify Christ's identity with the Father. The result was the enmity of the Arians, including the Emperor Constantius, who were intent on portraying Christ as similar (*homoiousios*) to the Father. He was exiled five times, including sojourns in Treves in Gaul and, finally, in Rome. It was a fortunate occurrence for the West and eventually for the universal church. For he spread the ascetical teachings of the Desert Fathers and was responsible for a great outburst of spirituality with his *Life of St. Anthony*. An apparently simple hagiographical exercise, this book fired an ascetical movement that affected men like Jerome, Augustine and Rufinus

[1]SC 199, 264-268.
[2]SC 199, 266.

and inspired people of all walks of life throughout the Roman empire.

The moral framework of Athanasius' thought reflects his fundamental notion of the Trinity. It sees the Son of God as the *Logos* or Word, both in the creation of mankind and in its redemption. He maintains that by departing from the *Logos*, men and women who are made in the image of the Word become intellectually blind and morally corrupt.

In his treatise *On the Incarnation*, Athanasius asserts that the true history of mankind consists in the life story of human beings created free and with a potentiality to happiness that depends on their capacity for deliberate choice. Improving on Aristotle's description of a fundamental option for free men, Athanasius maintains that all human beings, whether slave or free, enjoy this interior prerogative. Thus, the faculty for achieving felicity and enjoying freedom is based on God's guarantee given with the creation of man in the divine image. This freedom can be impaired by no outside power, though it is frequently abused from within the individual by sin and perversion. This has come about through the fall of Adam in paradise.

> The soul is fashioned according to the image of God ... Thus, when it discards the defilement of sin which covers it, and keeps only what is pure in that image, it is properly enlightened and beholds the Word as in a mirror since He is the image of the Father ... If the soul's own knowledge is deficient because of exterior distractions that becloud the mind and prevent its seeing what is above, it can still achieve a knowledge of God from the things that are seen. For creation, written, as it were, in characters of order and harmony, gives witness in a loud voice to its Master and Creator. *Against the Pagans* 34.3[3]

Athanasius then discusses the origin of sin as inevitably, though not necessarily, connected with the Incarnation.

[3]SC 18, 164.

Men, refusing to look at God in their negligence, devised and contrived evil for themselves and received the condemnation of death with which they had been threatened (in paradise). From then on they no longer continued in the manner in which they had been created; but they were corrupted by their own devices. Death then took control over them as a despot. For the breaking of the commandment turned them back to their natural state. Just as they had come into existence out of nothing, so they were rightly to expect the disintegration of their existence in the course of time. *On the Incarnation* 4.4[4]

However, Athanasius continues:

God not only made us out of nothing, but by the grace of his Word he freely endowed us with a divinely oriented life. Mankind, however, rejected the things of eternity and, prompted by the devil, turned to corruptible things. Thus, they became the reason for their own corruption in death. As I said before, mankind was by nature corruptible, but by the favor of communion in the Word, they were destined to escape the consequence of nature, if they had remained good. Because of the Word and His life among them, the natural corruption would not have affected them. *On the Incarnation* 5.1[5]

This conviction constituted, for Athanasius, the essence of human destiny.

While a champion of virginity, Athanasius gives a sample of his spiritual care for all his faithful:

Blessed are they who in their youth are joined in a free marriage and use nature for the begetting of offspring. We are of God's being (Acts 17:28), hence there is nothing

[4]SC 18, 215.
[5]SC 18, 216.

impure within us. Only then are we despoiled when we do
things of evil repute, namely sin ... There are some who
misuse the Gospel dictum, 'Not what enters but what
comes forth is what besmirches a man'...(Matthew
15:20). The Lord himself excludes ambiguity here by
adding 'what comes forth from the heart...' Doctors
describe for us the natural openings in the body...and
the Lord, who made them, tells us of their legitimate uses
when he says, 'Increase and multiply...' and the Apostle
speaks of 'an honorable union and unsullied bed'
(Hebrews 13:4)...Just as in war one must use discrimination in action so that what is not ordinarily licit becomes
such in the killing of the enemy...A similar reasoning
becomes the conjugal act. *Epistle to Amoun*[6]

It was with his highly spiritual concept of human destiny
that in his *Life of St. Anthony*, Athanasius captured the
fervor that animated the cenobitic movement of the age and
that he spread so effectively in the West. In the first section
he describes Anthony's decision to undertake an ascetical
life in the desert, his wisdom in dealing with the monks, the
persecution they suffered under Maximus Daja, as well as
the temptation to which he and his companions were subjected by the demons. He details Anthony's relations with
the Hellenic sages with whom he discussed philosophy, faith
and reason.

Athanasius began his moral instruction with practical
advice. Commenting on St. Paul's "I die daily," he says:

If we live each day as if we were about to die, we would
not sin. This is so to be understood, that daily on arising
we should imagine that we will not live until evening; and
when lying down, think we will not survive to get up
again. So disposed, if we live thus each day, we will not
sin, nor be held by cupidity, nor build up treasures on
earth ... We will forgive faults to everyone; nor will we

[6]PG 26, 1169-1173.

be detained by desire for women or evil pleasure ... always struggling with the day of judgment before us. *Life of Anthony* 19[7]

In encouraging his fellow monks to perseverence, he asserts:

> Let no one look back as did the wife of Lot ... Looking back is nought else but to be unhappy, once more hankering after ... worldly things ... Do not be afraid of the notion of virtue...for God is not far from us...The Greeks travel and cross the seas in order to learn letters... such journeys are not necessary for us. We do not have to travel or cross the seas, for the Kingdom of God is within us. By nature the soul is just, that is, intelligent by its creation. When, on the contrary, it declines from the right path, this is called vice. *Life of Anthony* 20[8]

On the psychological aspects of temptation, Athanasius advises:

> If the demons see Christians, and particularly monks, working and succeeding, they first try to attack by putting obstacles in the way, such as bad thoughts. But there is no need to be fearful about such suggestions ... For by prayer, fasting and faith in the Lord, they quickly disappear ... When indeed they cannot deceive the heart by their voluptuous obscenities, they approach by another way, and attempt to overcome with other distractions taking on the forms of women, animals, reptiles, immense bodies, armored monstrosities ... But neither are these exaggerated fantasies to terrorize us ... Since they are nothing, they quickly disappear if one arms himself with great faith and the sign of the cross. *Life of Anthony* 23[9]

[7]PG 26, 872.
[8]*Ibid.*
[9]PG 26, 876-877.

Speaking of the demons, Athanasius specifies:

> Demons are evil not because they were created such, for God has created no evil. They were made by God, but fell from the heavenly wisdom and, later, wrapped in the earth, they deceived the Gentiles by their wiles, and acted against us Christians with envy. There is nothing they do not attempt in order to prevent us from our entering into virtue. *Life of Anthony* 22[10]

In the religious and social context of the ancient world, the acceptance of the existence of demons capable of attacking the human consciousness was not strange nor infantile as it was portrayed by late nineteenth-century critics, such as Anatole France. It was merely a precursor of what Freud and modern psychiatrists have described as the fantasies and trauma resulting from the suppressed ills of the lower consciousness. Practical proof of the truth of this assertion lies in the remedy prescribed for this neurotic and psychologically ill by the desert spiritual directors: complete and unabashed revelation to a senior father who listened and, by indirection, aided the patient to self-mastery.

Basil of Caesarea

Born of an exemplary Christian family in Cappadocia, modern Turkey, Basil achieved renown as a bishop and theologian who vigorously defended orthodox doctrine, cared for the ill and impoverished, and pursued the freedom of the Church in its conflict with civil authority. Basil *pere* was a renowned rhetorician who had studied under Gregory, the wonder-worker, a disciple of Origen. Two of Basil's brothers, Gregory of Nyssa and Peter of Sebaste, are

[10]PG 26, 876.

honored as saints along with his mother, Emilia, and his sister, Macrina. Sent to Constantinople and Athens for his secular education, Basil met Gregory of Nazianzus, a fellow Cappadocian, and the two entered a life-long friendship. On his return to Cappadocia, Basil functioned as a rhetorician until his conversion to a more complete Christian life. Of his youthful manhood he writes:

> Addicted for a long time to vanity, I wasted almost the whole of my youth in useless occupations. I was employed in studying the disciplines of a wisdom that is foolish in God's sight when suddenly, as it were, I awakened from sleep and saw the luminous light of the Gospel truth. I suddenly realized the inutility of the principles of the wisdom of the world. *Epistle* 2:23[11]

Despite the exaggeration of this disclaimer regarding his worldly education, Basil profitted greatly by the experience and knowledge he thus acquired. In later life he was to write an *Address to Youth* as a justification of the use of the pagan learning in delineating the Christian creed. Meanwhile he confessed:

> Greatly deploring my miserable life, I sought after a discipline that would familiarize me with the truths of religion. Above all, I wanted a change by way of an emendation of my morals which a long familiarity with evil-doers had perverted. Then, when I read the Gospels, I found everywhere that many things led to perfection including divesting oneself of possessions, consorting with the poor and in need, and not being over-concerned with this life, nor wasting affection on the things of the world. *Ibid.*

Attracted at first to the highly ascetical practices of Eustathius of Sebaste, Basil soon discovered discrepancies

[11]PG 32, 823.

between the rigorism of this movement and the benevolence of the Gospel. Breaking with the Eustathian community, he started out on a *Wanderjahr* to discover the sources of the ascetical movement being pursued by the monks of the desert.

> And I found many in Alexandria and the rest of Egypt, many more in Palestine, and Coelosyria, and in Mesopotamia, whose frugality in taking food and whose dedication to work amazed me. I marvelled at their constancy in prayer, how they overcame sleep and were not disturbed by the lack of natural necessities; how they persevered in a constant and indomitable frame of mind in hunger and thirst, in cold and nudity; never favoring their bodies nor voluntarily giving it care. And while I wondered at these things and began to consider the life of such men blessed as they carried in their bodies the mortification of Jesus, I myself began to desire to imitate these people. *Ibid.*[12]

On his return to Caesarea, Basil was baptized and embarked on an ascetical life on the family estate of Annesos, near the villa of his mother and aunt Macrina on the banks of the Iris River. He was joined in this pursuit by Gregory of Nazianzus. Discussing this period of his life, Basil wrote:

> While there are many things about which I should weep, on one thing I dare to boast in the Lord. Namely that I never had erroneous ideas about God. Nor did I think otherwise after I had been instructed. The notion of God that I received as a boy from my holy mother and my aunt Macrina, I retained as it grew in me. Nor have I changed it in any way when reasoning took over. The principles they imparted to me I have adhered to. *Letter 223, 3*[13]

[12]PG 32, 823.
[13]PG 32, 826.

With this as the foundation of his faith, Basil was to write a definitive treatise on the Holy Spirit that was crucial at the Council of Constantinople in 381 in the definition of the third person of the Trinity as divine, equal to the Father and the Son.

In one of his first literary endeavors, aided by Gregory, Basil prepared a series of answers based directly on scriptural texts in reply to moral dilemmas placed before him by the ascetical men and women of Cappadocia. This treatise, called his *Moralia*, was followed by a work known as the *Asceticon*. It was published in two versions knows as the Longer and Shorter Rules.

Basil inaugurates his reflection on what is good by insisting that true goodness reflects godliness and as such must be the equivalent of blessedness.

> That is blessed that is good in itself. It is the center of all that exists—inimitable in its nature, of royal dignity, untouched by the vicissitudes of life, happy in its manner of life, impervious to alteration and change.

> Ignorant men, he maintains, loving the world, who do not know the nature of goodness, often value things for naught—riches, health, the splendor of life in which there is nothing by its nature that is good. *Homily on Psalm 1, 3*[14]

As if suddenly realizing the full importance of what he was saying for the entire Christian community, Basil continues:

> But why does David the prophet select only the men to call him blessed? Are women to be excluded from goodness? Let it not be. They who share the same nature have the same spiritual capability and achievement. *Ibid.*

[14]PG 29, 215.

In keeping with the classic Christian anthropology, Basil maintains:

> We indeed have a soul and a mind in as far as we have been created in God's image. But we also have a body to which are attached the senses. And round about us are the necessities of life—money, the arts, and other furnishings of life. And what does Scripture tell us? Do not be overconcerned about your flesh, nor pursue its good health, the beauty of pleasurable enjoyment, a long life, money or glory . . . Look to yourself and your soul. *Ibid.*

In dealing with the notion of evil, Basil says:

> It is necessary to insist that God is not the author of evil since nothing contrary can be generated from its contrary. Life does not beget death, nor is darkness the principle of light: nor sickness the tool of health. Hence if evil is neither ungenerated nor born of God, whence does it arise? For no one alive denies that evil exists. What then? Evil is not a livng substance, nor is it animated. But it is an affection of the mind contrary to virtue . . . *Hom. 24 in Hexameron*[15]

Of original sin:

> Thus if the Lord had not come in the flesh, the Redeemer could not have paid the price of our death. For if there is anything that is subject to the command of death, it is something assured by the Lord. Death does not cease to carry out what belongs to it. *Letter 261, 2*[16]

The original edition of Basil's *Asceticon*, preserved in the Latin translation of Rufinus of Aquileia, was written while

---

[15] PG 29, 38-39; SC 26 bis, 158.
[16] PG 32, 970.

Basil was still a priest evangelizing the Cappadocian country-side. It consists of the actual answers to questions put to him by members of the Christian community. To the body of practical queries, Basil supplied a sort of proemium in the first eleven questions, laying down the principles he considered fundamental to the evangelical *ascesis*. The moral doctrine of the *Asceticon* reflects the original *Regulae morales*. There is a call to penance and conversion in the spirit of John the Baptist, but immediate emphasis is turned to the love of God in keeping with Christ's enunciation of the two great commandments. Basil clarifies the pertinence of this basic religious obligation with a philosophical reflection on the fact that human nature is obviously made for knowledge in relation to the absolute good, and with an insistence that man can only live in society. In questions eight and nine of the original *Asceticon*, he summarizes the Christian moral teaching under the title of continence.

Little of Basil's philosophical formation betrays itself in his *Regulae*, other than in the questions where a general awareness of the Stoic and Neo-Platonic psychology underlies the fashion in which he deals with virtues and vices. Basil accepts the Platonic structure of human psychology with the body as primarily the receptacle for the soul, and the source of its griefs in unruly passions and emotions. In subsequent works, particularly in his *Homilies on the Psalms*, Basil employed his training as a rhetorician to work out a philosophical foundation for the Christian moral teaching that one could discover in the wisdom of King David — the presumed author of the Psalms. It is obvious that the *Nicomachean Ethics* of Aristotle are not far from his thoughts as he distinguished between the *paideia* of the prophets and that of the Old Law more generally. Basil compares the moral formation contained in the Psalms to the humanistic education provided by the study of medicine that offers proper treatment for every kind of disease and trauma.

In dealing with the sinner and wrong-doer, Basil shows a truly evangelical understanding and compassion:

Wisely and sufficiently intelligent is the invitation to virtue through a diminishing of vice. It is not possible to strive for perfection from the start. Nor is it right to tell someone still given to evil doing that he should do good; rather he should be encouraged to recede from vice. For it is only when he has had his full of wrong-doing that he becomes capable of doing good and becoming involved with good works ... *Homily on Psalm* 1, 4[17]

Basil continues in this realistic appraisal:

There is in human affairs a true justice and a simulated justice. On this topic many secular writers have left treatises. But since what is truly God's authentic justice is ignored by these people, they were not able to produce anything really worthy of human justice. Thus the laws of diverse people are different, even contrary in many aspects, because the laws of true justice were not achieved by them. For example, parricide is accepted as just by certain people. Among others an incestuous union is considered somehow a more sacred kind of matrimony ... Likewise the examination of justice cannot be perceived in each equally since some sins are committed with the will and others against one's will ... Thus, for example, if someone educated a child who entered this world through wicked and unjust parents by whom his mind was infected with wicked and evil words and deeds and developed evil ways, while another had many occasions in which he was integrated to virtue, through the honest instruction of nurses, the grave stricture of his parents with knowledge of the divine Word, if after all this, the latter commits a crime similar to that of the former, should he not be burdened with a greater punishment even though the guilt of wrong-doing is the same? *Ibid.*[18]

[17]PG 29, 218.
[18]PG 29, 239.

Basil's final exhortation to both the individual and the community deals with meekness, obedience, poverty, temperance, fraternal charity, the cause and cure for evil thoughts and bad dreams, the obligation to forgive slights on the part of one's brethren, and the general method of dealing with delinquents. He encourages all to reveal their inmost thoughts to a spiritual director, thus to avoid morbidity and self-indulgence; but he provides no specific information for solving current problems regarding the nature of auricular confession in the early church.

It is in his sermons, particularly those delivered in the aftermath of the great famine that devastated Cappadocia in 367, that Basil's moral teaching on social and economic justice is most effectively expressed. When the civil authorities proved inadequate before this emergency, Basil, though still only a priest, assumed responsibility for organizing subscriptions, forcing merchants to open their granaries, and setting up canteens in the public squares. He then mounted the pulpit to thunder against the avarice and rapaciousness of speculators and exploiters. Basil lays down blunt moral principles concerning the nature of man's tenure of private property and the necessities of life.

> What you call your own is not yours in the way you suppose. You did not bring it into the world. You rich are like a man who would keep all others out of a theatre, using what was intended for all as his exclusively, simply because he was the first to arrive. *Homily in Time of Famine*[19]

He is driving home the truth that every man has an inalienable right to a living; that in the case of conflict, private rights must cede to common needs.

[19]PG 31, 275.

> Is not the man who robs another of his clothing called a
> thief? But is the man who is able to clothe the naked, and
> refuses, deserving of any other appellation? The bread
> that you withhold belongs to the hungry. The cloak that
> you retain in your chest belongs to the naked. The gold
> that you have hidden in the ground belongs to the indi-
> gent. Therefore, as often as you were able to help others
> and refused, so often did you do them wrong. *Ibid.*

Basil's denunciation of extravagance and avarice follows
the fashion of the Old Testament prophets at well as the
Cynic-Stoic diatribes of the ancient moralist. He indulges a
commomplace in exposing the extravagance and folly of
"proud and whimsical women" who fall into excessive luxury, and are never satisfied. Every day they follow a new
fancy. "I must have" they say, "expensive dresses, gold vases
... and gorgeous uniforms for the servants ... " But he is no
less severe on her male counterpart. "You say you will not
contribute; that you have not enough to satisfy all who beg
from you. Your tongue swears, but your hand refutes it
utterly ... by the stone in the ring flashing all round your
finger."

Much ink was wasted earlier in this century on the problem whether Basil was advocating communism. What he
was inculcating was a communitarian society after the ideal-
ized model portrayed in the New Testament, and particularly in the early stages of the Acts of the Apostles. He could
hardly be on more solidly Christian grounds.

Basil flushed out his preaching by an enterprise of social
action remarkable for its practicality and compassion for
the poor, the deprived and the desolate. He began by setting
up, close to his own cathedral city, a large house of hospitality, into which he welcomed, cared for, and comforted the
ill, the poor, the aged and the stranger. The project pros-
pered. In a short time it grew into a veritable city of charity.
For, adding a separate building for his own residence, he
soon saw the necessity of a dwelling for his priests. This in
turn was followed by a nurses' home, a hospice for pilgrims,

a house of convalescence; then workshops, stables, granaries and guild-houses. When he stopped and looked about him, he had a whole new city to show for his labors. Nor was his grateful flock slow in acknowledging the work as distinctive of Basil's genius. They named this foundation of mercy a "*basiliad.*"

In discussing the care for the children entrusted to the monastic-like home, either by their parents, or relatives, or friends of orphaned or abandoned youngsters, Basil laid down a series of considerations that have a very modern ring. Thus, in the area of child psychology, his observation reflect a blend of the classical pedagogy with his own blend of moralism. He encourages the ascetical communities to accept orphans and abandoned children. In regard to those presented by their parents, however, he cautions that they should only be received in the presence of numerous witnesses, to forestall possible future parental complaints or claims. His primary interest is in the proper formation of the child's character; and his knowledge of human nature is such as to encompass a wide variety of traits and temperments. He believes in the rod as a pedagogic aid; its use, however, is to be exercised only by a benevolent master in full control of himself and his charges. Ordinarily, corrective measures should reflect the fault committed. Has the child been angry or overbearing with his companions? He should be encouraged to make this up in retributive kindnesses. Such humiliation will cure the spirit of a tendency to anger that is so frequently caused by pride. If he eats outside the regular times, or without moderation, he should be made to fast throughout a good part of the day. Should he be guilty of foul language, unkind conduct, lying, or other forbidden actions, "silence and fasting will help him come to his senses." G. Bardy discusses whether Basil had in mind a type of secular education for these youngsters. The problem was prompted by question 292 of the small *Asceticon.* But Basil's answer is vague. He uses the word *didaskalos* (teacher), but does not seem to have had in mind the teaching of grammar and rhetoric.

In their overall guidance, Basil ordained that children should be separated both by sex and age from the older members of the community. Not only should they have more sleep and a diet of their own, but they should be allowed time and space to make noise and to play, without disturbing other members of the community. He does not want them scandalized by the faults of the older inhabitants. They have no way of knowing, he says, that an adult who is a child mentally will behave childishly. He prescribes that they be imbued with the edifying stories and heroic deeds performed by the saints in the Scriptures rather than taught the salacious myths of the gods and heroes of classical literature.

On the question of women's rights, Basil did not measure up to modern standards or even those of his contemporary and friend, Gregory of Nazianzus. He admitted that the Savior's command against divorce, except for fornication, applied equally to men and women; but he advised that both secular and ecclesiastical custom justified discrimination against woman, demanding that she tolerate a husband who indulged in fornication or adultery. "Hence I do not know whether a woman who lives with a man dismissed by his wife should be called an adulteress," Basil temporizes. He contends that, in the Church's tradition, a woman should stay with her husband, even though he maltreated her, with the hope that she might convert him, particularly if he were an infidel, in keeping with St. Paul's admonition (1 Cor. 7:16). The woman abandoned is worthy of tolerance by the church: and whoever lives with her is not to be condemned as an adulterer. But the man who abandons his wife is an adulterer, and she who cohabits with him comes under the same condemnation.

This contention shocked Gregory of Nazianzus who reacted with pained remonstrance. In this matter, he maintained, many were badly disposed and professed a law that was both evil and inconsistent.

How can they coerce the wife and indulge the husband? The woman is threatened with the most cruel punishment ... but the man who violates the faith given to his wife is liable to no punishment. This law I do not approve ... It is men who sanction such laws, and carry them out against women ... But God does not act in this fashion. The one creator of man and woman, he has brought both out of the same dust, with one image, one law, one death, and one resurrection. *Oration* 37, 6[20]

It was Rufinus of Aquileia who at the turn of the fifth century introduced Basil to the West — and he did so to disseminate his influence as a moralist as well as an ascetical guide. During Lent of 398, he translated Basil's small *Asceticon* for abbot Ursacius and the monastic community near Terracina called Pinetum. Then, in 400 or 401, he dedicated his Latin translation of eight Basilian sermons to Apronianus and Avita, with the observation:

This I would like you to know. Basil's style, in the fineness of his Greek speech and his grace of expression, is very similar to that of our Cyprian, from whom indeed, in the worthiness of his life, he does not greatly differ ... Cyprian acquired the primary palm for his confession as a martyr ... Basil was crowned with the martyrdom of a ceaseless conscience, each day and moment opposing luxury with sobriety, passion with virginity, wrath with meekness, and pride with humility. His work is thus more moral in nature, fit for guiding souls toward the good life, and relieving them in their labors ... Its perusal will be found most suitable for religiously minded women ... since it is not burdened with questions of a dogmatic nature ... *Preface to Homilies of Basil*[21]

[20]PG 36, 290.
[21]CCL 20, 237.

One could hardly provide a more fitting or just appraisal of Basil as a moralist.

Gregory of Nazianzus

Gregory of Nazianzus was a student and ascetic companion of St. Basil. Of almost the same age and family background, both men were educated in the Hellenic tradition in Constantinople and Athens. In keeping with the ecclesial practice of the times, they were baptized in their early twenties, having presumably outgrown their youthful vices. More of an ascetic than a political churchman, Gregory was reluctantly ordained a priest by his father. In the midst of factional disputes he was chosen as Bishop of Constantinople in 381 by a majority of the people and presided over the first Council of Constantinople that defined the divinity of the Holy Spirit. Disgusted with the incessant theological disputes that disturbed the city, Gregory resigned his See and returned to Nazianzus.

Speaking of the atmosphere that prevailed in Constantinople at the time, Gregory of Nyssa says:

> You enter a bakeshop and ask for bread. Instead of selling you the bread, the baker wants to talk to you about the 'begotten' and the 'unbegotten' Son. The cashier will argue that the Father is greater than the Son. And if you desire a bath, the custodian will assure you that the Son surely proceeds from nothing ... [22]

Forty-one of Gregory's major Homilies are preserved, including his Five Theological Orations delivered in Constantinople in the fall of 380 to vindicate the orthodoxy of

[22]PG 46, 557.

the Nicene Creed. Insisting on the majesty and importance
of theology, Gregory maintains:

> It is not the prerogative of anyone to discourse about
> God. Not anyone, I say, for this is not a common matter
> proper to the earth-bound. Rather, it is incumbent on
> those who have explored the subject with great exactness
> and after deep meditation . . . and who so proceed after
> purging themselves of all vices . . . *Oration 27*[23]

His Apology for his flight contains a complete treatise on
the priesthood that was used by John Chrysostom in his *Six
Books on the Priesthood*. In Gregory's *On His Own Life*, he
supplies an autobiography that compares favorably with
Augustine's *Confessions*.

In Gregory's thought, mankind is considered the consummation of creation. It is the result of an eternal contemplation:

> The Father solicitous to discover a creature who would
> contemplate His Wisdom, the source of all being, and
> who is King, similar to God, decided: Behold since the
> servants of pure immaterial nature (angels) already
> occupy the heavens and proclaim my glory forever . . .
> The earth, thus far, has only beings without reason . . . It
> pleases me to create a new race composed of two ele-
> ments: a being endowed with reason, who occupies space
> between the mortal and the immortal; man capable of
> enjoying my works with a heart that will initiate itself in
> celestial things, with power over the things of the world.
> (God) taking in his immortal hands a bit of the newly
> formed earth gave it the form of my being by which he
> made me a part of his own life. In effect he breathed into
> me a spirit which emanated from his invisible divinity. Of
> the earth and of God's breathing, I have been formed, me,

[23]SC 250, 76.

> a man, me, the image of the immortal ... This is the
> reason I have this life, because of the earth in which I am
> formed and I guard in my heart the desire of that other
> life, because of sharing the divine ... *Poem* I.1.8[24]

While Gregory points to this idealistic picture of mankind
reflecting the divinization predicated in the Platonic theology, he is also conscious of the other aspect of human life.
He sees mankind living on three levels: that of flesh and
blood; that of the spirit through the water of baptism; and
that of repentance. While Gregory has left us clear teaching
about the effect of original sin on the individual human
being, he does describe mankind:

> The soul of man never ceases to deplore his painful
> slavery, the error of our first parents, the culpable seduc-
> tion of our mother (Eve) who became the mother of our
> concupiscense, the lying perfidy of the torturous serpent
> thirsty for our blood, who rejoices over the sins of man-
> kind, the words, the fruit of the pernicious tree for
> mortals, the faultful appetite that opened the gate to
> death, the shameful nudity of its members and the exclu-
> sion without glory from pardon and the tree of life ...
> *Poem* 45[25]

While Gregory attributes the substance of man's rebellion
to Satan, he places a particular burden on the woman who
for the sake of the tree of knowledge deprived mankind of
the tree of life. He attributes to Eve more than a mere
deception by the devil. He feels there was pride and bad will
on her part. Nevertheless, he discusses sinfulness in the
tradition of Irenaeus as the result of a childish impatience
that God allowed Adam to indulge.

[24]PG 37, 451.

[25]PG 37, 1360.

This being He placed in paradise — whatever that paradise may have been (having honoured him with the gift of free will, in order that good might belong to him as the result of his choice, no less than to Him Who had implanted the seeds of it) ... And He gave Him a Law, as material for his free will to act upon. This Law was a commandment as to what plants he might partake of and which one he might not touch. This latter was the Tree of Knowledge; not, however, because it was evil from the beginning when planted; nor was it forbidden because God grudged it to men — let not the enemies of God wag their tongues in that direction, or imitate the serpent. But it would have been good if partaken at the proper time; for the Tree was, according to my theory, Contemplation, which it is only safe for those who have reached maturity of habit to enter upon; but which is not good for those who are still somewhat simple and greedy; just as neither is solid food good for those who are yet tender and have need of milk. But when through the devil's malice and the woman's caprice, to which she succumbed as the more tender, and which she brought to bear upon the man, as she was the more apt to persuade — alas for my weakness, for that of my first father was mine; he forgot the commandment which had been given him, and yielded to the baleful fruit; and for his sin was banished at once form the tree of life, and from paradise, and from God.[26]

Hence, the desire to achieve this knowledge amounted to *hubris*. With St. Paul, then Gregory sees all mankind under the dominion of sinfulness (Romans 5:12). But where Origen and Gregory of Nyssa seek an explanation of this phenomenon, Gregory of Nazianzus merely states the fact. In the final analysis, it is the devil who prevails in subjecting mankind to temptation.

[26]PG 36, 632; cf. NPNF 7 ser. 2, 425.

Gregory provides a realistic psychological description of temptation:

> About sunset, I used to go for a walk by myself along the seashore. This is what I have always done when I want to relax and take my mind off my troubles. While my feet were carrying me along, I kept my eyes fixed on the sea. I found no delight in it, though at other times, when its calm surface turns a deep red and it laps against the shore in sweet and gentle paly, it is most delightful. But at that particular time (I take delight in adding the words of Scripture) the sea *arose* in agitation *by reason of a great wind that blew.* (Jn. 6:18) And, as usually happens in such storms, some of the waves began to swell far out at sea and, after gradually reaching a crest, rippled to the shore and died, while others crashed over the nearby rocks and were sent flying backwards and dissipated in foam and fine mist. Truly, I said, is not our life, and human affairs in general, an ocean that contains much bitterness and instability? And are not the winds the temptations that befall us and all the unexpected turns of events that occur? It seemed to me that people subjected to temptation fall into two groups: some are swept away like objects that are exceeding light and lifeless without putting up the least resistance to the assaults made against them: they have not in themselves the means to resist, no ballast of prudence and reason to withstand the accidents of fate; others are a *rock* worthy of that Rock on which we stand and which we worship, that is, all those who adopt a philosophic mode of life and rise above the ordinary forms of humility. They stand firm before all attacks, steadfast and unshaken. *Or.* 26, pg 35.1237[27]

[27]Or. 26, PG 35, 1237.

Gregory stresses further the need for grace.

> Even to desire well needs the aid of God; even to choose
> what is right is a divine gift due to God's mercy. It is
> necessary that we both act of our own accord as masters
> and at the same time have our salvation from God ...

Gregory cites the Psalm "Unless the Lord build the
house" to insist that along with fasting, penitence in tears,
vigils and constant prayer, God's accompanying assistance
is necessary. But then he pauses to rule out a crude predesti-
nationism:

> I fear lest some monstrous reasoning be brought up, such
> as that the soul pre-existed somewhere else before being
> bound to its present body and that from that other life it
> has received the gift of philosophy while others are con-
> demned ... *Oration* 37.13[28]

Gregory takes from Philo Judaus his teaching on *theoria*
and *praxis* — contemplation and action — along with a
katharsis or interior cleansing of the soul. While he failed to
consider the 'evangelical counsels' as they were elaborated
in the West with Tertullian and Cyprian, he did conceptual-
ize the notions of virginity and chastity, elevating them far
beyond the mere abstention from sexual pleasure. In a
funeral oration for his sister Gorgonia, he distinguishes:

> In regard to the two divisions of life, the married and the
> virginal state, while the latter is more lofty and of divine
> origin, it is more difficult and dangerous. The former is
> more humble and safer...(The latter requires) becoming
> modest without pride, blending the excellence of both
> states and providing that neither binds us to God abso-

[28]PG 36, 297; cf. LNPF 7, 342.

> lutely or separates us from the world ... It is a mind that presides over both virginity and wedlock. Under the master hand of reason, it works on them as raw material for virtue. *Oration* 8.8[29]

In the end Gregory explains the life of the Christian as surrounded by doubts and difficulties despite a determination to live constantly in Christ.

> The good ground brings forth good fruit in patience. The good we do is without value unless at the same time we bear in patience the evil-doing of our neighbors. And the higher anyone ascends in virtue, the harder will this world bear down on him. For the more the love of the heart turns from this present life the more the opposition of this world mounts up. Hence, it is that we see so many strive after and do that which is good; yet they exist under the burden of afflictions. For though they have turned away from earthly things, they are yet harassed with increasing tribulation. But according to the Word of the Lord, they shall bring forth fruit in patience; and after their time of tribulation, they shall be received into the rest above. *Oration* 4

John Chrysostom (350-407)

The most renowned of the Greek Fathers as preacher and moralist was John Chrysostom — the 'Golden mouth' — who as orator and bishop of Antioch in Syria was selected by the Emperor Theodosius to be the Patriarch of Constantinople only to run foul of the "pope" of Alexandria, the Patriarch Theophilus, and the Empress Eudoxia. Unjustly condemned by the Synod of the Oak in 403, he was exiled to the Caucuses where he died in 407. A prodigious preacher,

[29]PG 36, 797.

John left behind an enormous heritage of scripture commentaries, tracts, letters and sermons that cover the whole
of the Old and New Testaments.

In his six books *On the Priesthood*, he models himself on
Gregory of Nazianzus' *Treatise on his Flight* and provides
us with a close look into the daily life of Antioch in the
fourth century. In the first section, he describes his student
days and his friendship with Basil of Antioch who felt the
call to an ascetical life and wanted Chrysostom to join him.

> While our friendship remained firm — we had expe-
> rienced the same schooling, the same companions and
> outlook — our interests gradually varied...Good as he
> was he made much of our friendship.
> *On the Priesthood* [30]

Chrysostom then describes his mother's anguish on discovering his intention to retreat from the world and live as a
hermit in a mountain cave. In his poignant description of
her plight he reveals the circumstances of life faced by a
widow of her station in the well-to-do society of Antioch.

> When my mother learned of my agreement (to become a
> monk), she led me by the hand into her bedroom and told
> me to sit down beside the bed on which I had been
> brought into life. Then amid her tears she said: 'I was not
> given by divine providence to enjoy your father's protec-
> tion for very long. With the pains of your birth I was
> faced with his death leaving you prematurely an orphan
> and me a widow. It is only one who has experienced the
> perils of widowhood who can describe them. No speech
> can depict the storm and cyclone which a young woman
> undergoes when having only recently left her father's
> house with no skill in business affairs and suddenly
> stricken with an unbearable grief, she is forced to under-
> take obligations greater than her age and sex. She has to

[30]SC 272, 60.

correct the evil ways of the servants, recognize and repel the evil intentions of her relatives, the molestations of tax gatherers and, with strength, confront the savagery of their demands.

And if the dead man has left a child, should it be a girl, she will exhibit great care for her mother sharing her possessions and fears. But if a son, he will fill her with innumerable worries and cares, and she is forced to incur great expense if she wants to obtain a liberal education for him.

His mother continued the account of her plight:

Nothing then could persuade me to enter a second marriage and bring into your father's home a new spouse. But I continued amid the storm and whirlwind. I did not evade the terrors of my widowhood strengthened in the first place by divine grace; then experiencing the consolation of looking on your face where the living image of the dead one was so accurately reproduced. Nor can anyone accuse me of wrongdoing in this. For while I bore my widowhood with strength, I did not diminish your inheritance through the inconveniences of widowhood which unhappily I have seen happen to many orphans. For your liberal education I used my own means and what I had brought with me from my father's house. Do not think I am scolding you in so saying. But for all this I ask one favor. Do not make me a widow a second time. Await my death. When you confine me to the earth close to your father's remains, you can take on your lengthy journeyings. For though you say you are loved by so many others, no one can grant you the liberty I have given you. *On the Priesthood*[31]

It is a touching picture of the tribulation to which a young widow was subject. Despite his eloquence in describing her

[31]SC 272, 66.

plight and tearful request that he not desert her, John did retire to the desert for several years. On his return, he was ordained a deacon and then a priest in Antioch.

In his Homilies on Paul's Epistle to the Romans, Chrysostom plumbs the depths of the problem of sin.

> How has death contrived to dominate life? By the fault of one man. That is the meaning of (Paul's) "In whom we have sinned." By his (Adam's) fault, all others, even though innocent of partaking of the tree, have been made mortal. When he says further that sin was in the world down to the coming of the law, it seems to me that he is saying that once the Law was given (to Moses), the sin that arose through transgression was in possession. It remained dominant while the Law prevailed. For he says that without the Law there is no sin. If, therefore, you say, that sin brought us death by transgression of the Law, how is it that those who lived before the Law have all died? Hence it seems clear that it is not sin itself that is the transgressor but it was Adam's sin of disobedience that brought about his loss and all with him. *Homily 10 on Romans*[32]

Further meditating on Paul's assertion that Adam is a type of Christ,

> How can there be sin when we have so great a teacher? With death a congeries of passions entered. When the body became mortal it was subjected to concupiscence, wrath, sorrow and other evils that must be controlled by reason lest they submerge us in the depth of sinfulness. These affections are not sinful in themselves; but unless curbed their inordinate use brings on sin. For example, concupiscence is not a sin. But if it becomes immoderate; if, not content within the law of marriage, one seeks after other women, then it gives rise to adultery. It is not

concupiscence as such but the unrestrained desire that is indulged. Sin arises from a corrupt judgment and contentiousness rather than from avidity. It is not of the flesh as heretics contend. Sins of concupiscence arise from the soul and mind and this is the fount of all evils. After the mind becomes a reprobate, one's character being corrupted, all else goes wrong. *Homily 11 on Romans*[33]

In his sermons and scripture commentaries delivered mainly in homiletic fashion, Chrysostom routinely utilized the diatribe characteristic of the second sophistic rhetoric that formed the substance of his secular education. Thus, his discourses are really a dialexis in which he uses all the techniques of oratorical competence; feigning audience participation, proposing and answering objections and denials, employing popular speech, addressing children to demonstrate the juvenile behavior of their parents, and describing concrete situations in the everyday affairs of professional life, labor, sports, family ambitions and foibles, the gamut of medical experiences, clerical and monastic life, the theatre, politics, and profligacy. Behind these rhetorical devices is a Platonic anthropology that divides the soul into three parts: reason, the irascible and the concupiscible faculties.

Chrysostom accepted this pattern and adapted it to the anthropological insights contained in the Sacred Scriptures. Thus, he insists that, in the Sermon on the Mount, Christ was reinforcing the obligations of the decalogue by attacking the roots of evil doing, whereas Moses has merely condemned external sins. Chrysostom then gives a resume of the Beatitudes according to the Stoic schema:

"You see," he says, "how Jesus eradicates anger;
then the concupiscence of the body, of money,
and of glory. ... For he who is poor, who is meek,
and who weeps (the first three beatitudes) has
conquered wrath. He who is just and merciful (beatitudes
4 and 5) roots out evil desires.

[33]PG 60.

> And he who is persecuted, insulted, and despised
> (beatitudes 8 and 9) practices detachment from
> earthly goods, and will be purified of all vanity
> and ambition." *Homily 13 on Matthew*[34]

Finding no place for the peace-makers in the Stoic schema, he simply drops this beatitude from consideration. But in utilizing the topos of the diatribe, he makes a psychological synthesis demonstrating the evils that are connected with irascibility and concupiscence. He divides the latter into an avidity for a) possessions; b) sexual pleasure, c) gluttony and d) ambition. It is here that John makes his own contribution to the psychological insights of the day. He rejects as inhuman and unnecessary the Stoic attempt to supress the passions. Reflecting on the fact that Christ experienced anger, that he wept and frequently demonstrated compassion, Chrysostom concluded that the passions were to be controlled and used with measure—*metriopatheia*. The Stoics, he says, preached mildness and patience, and Plato condemned the idea of returning evil for evil. Nevertheless, in the final analysis Chrysostom maintained that while the pagan philosophers achieved moral excellence, the Christians:

> "are called to a more perfect life. We seek a higher ideal,
> and strive in a more difficult arena of combat. The life to
> which we are called is one of virtue in accord with a divine
> message . . . "[35]

For this reason Chrysostom insisted that the ideal of evangelical perfection was for all — for the laity as well as for monks, for the clergy and virgins. He says explicitly that perfection is not based upon the difficulty of virtuous acts, for "God does not demand the same degree of virtue from all." It is rather an attitude of mind that includes faith and love. Chrysostom likewise insists that true perfection is not

[34]PG 57, 212.
[35]PG 52, 510.

achieved by the practical or juridical observance of the evangelical precepts; nor does it lead to an infallible certainty of salvation.

Thus, monasticism is only one path to perfection:

> The beatitudes announced by Christ are not reserved exclusively for monks. For this could imply the condemnation of the rest of the world; and we could reasonably accuse God of cruelty. If the beatitudes were only for monks, if the worldly had no hope of achieving them, God himself, by permitting people to marry, would have lost the human race.[36]

While he admitted a distinction between the precepts and the counsels, because both Christ and St. Paul had indicated a difference, he would not allow the laity to conclude that the precepts alone were for them:

> Have the monks alone the duty of pleasing God? Certainly not. God wishes that all become holy and not neglect any virtue.[37]

He insisted that people in the world should strive for perfection according to the monastic ideal by practising prayer and contemplation, beginning with meditation on the sacred scriptures.

> The spiritual grapplings, the meditated readings, the vigils, and fasting; why do we propose these things to non-monks? Do not ask me. Run to St. Paul who gives us this admonition: *Watch in all patience, and pray* (Col. 4, 2); *Stop giving attention to your sinful nature to satisfy its desires* (Rom. 13, 14). This was not written for monks alone; but for all who live in the world. For the layman

[36]PG 63, 67.
[37]PG 53, 182.

has no more than the monk, except that he lives with his wife. This is the sole difference. In all else he is bound to the same obligations.[38]

Chrysostom likewise insists on the individual's responsibility to use his free will in accord with God's suggestions, stating explicitly that God has tempered his commands with mildness, allowing us to act not because of his precepts, but of our own free will. Although they are worthy of chastisement, God even accepts the obedience of those who are faithful merely out of fear (Homily on 1 Cor. 21. 5:16).

But a fundamental rule of the Christian way of life is service to one's neighbor. God has made all men brothers, so that the interest of one is the interest of all. Hence, no one can bring his own affairs into order without providing for the love and salvation of his neighbor.

> Many imagine that it suffices for their virtue to assure their own salvation; and that in regulating their lives honestly, they lack nothing. This is an error, as the parable of the talents shows ... Do not think it is enough to work for your own welfare, for thus you can run to ruin.[39]

He thus condemned flight into the desert as a dereliction from the obligations of the Christian, and a return to the selfishness of the pagan philosophy. Not even the motive of "Not to lose myself, not to become less vigorous in virtue," was justified in Chrysostom's thinking. He maintained that it was much better to lose fervor in virtue while taking care of others, than to achieve the heights of contemplation, but to regard one's perishing neighbors with indifference. For him a self-centered or egotistical seeking of salvation was impossible:

[38]PG 63, 68.
[39]PG 58, 601.

> You can continue fasting, sleep on the ground, eat cinders, weep without cease. But if you are not useful to others, you are doing nothing worthwhile.[40]

Chrysostom spoke frequently on marriage, its joys and tribulations. As an accomplished satirist, he followed a tradition of both pagan and Christian exaggeration that gave rise to the impression that he had misogynistic tendencies and misconstrued the nature of Christian marriage. Actually he projects a very healthy attitude. Speaking of the end of marriage:

> Before all else learn what is the reason for sexual relations and why it was introduced in a life of togetherness. ... Listen to Paul who tells us "each one has a wife in order to avoid fornication" (1 Cor. 7:2). He does not say to avoid poverty and give rise to riches. What then? In order to avoid sinfulness; to moderate our desires so that we may live soberly and please God, content with one's own wife. This is what life together will bring us and this is its fruit and gain. In this fashion a fervid and genuine love is brought into being; all unchasteness is eliminated; and so one loving his wife has no other desires than legitimate pleasure; from innocent and proper love and through chasteness capturing the favor of the divine being. ...[41]

Nor is Chrysostom unaware of the daily concerns of ordinary people.

> Why talk to me about the beauty of the body? That you may learn about its outstanding chasteness and the pulchritude of the mind? For the actuality of chasteness is to be taken up all the more if it is conjoined with an exceptional beauty of the body. Beauty is not necessarily the cause of fornication, nor is deformity the guarantee of

[40]PG 62, 698, 68, 480.
[41]PG 51, 232.

> continence. Many who are noted for their bodily pulchritude are made more illustrious through their chasteness while others of ugly men become ugly also in soul through fornication. In each case the cause is the intention of the mind not the nature of the body.[42]

Chrysostom asserts the equality of the spouses in their marital state.

> Why does Paul say the woman does not have power over her own body? He is acknowledging a great equality. As the man is the lord of his own body, she is also the mistress of his body. Why then has he introduced so great an equality of honor? For indeed this consideration is very necessary. Where there is concern for chastity and chasteness, the man has nothing the woman does not have, but he is held to the same discipline as she, if he should violate the laws of marriage, and this properly. For the woman does not come to you, leaving her father and all else to have you treat her with contumely.[43]

Chrysostom's moral teaching is the direct result of his experience as a young man, annealed by an all-embracing love of Christ that he achieved during his flight into the desert and his monastic experience. His return to the world does not seem to have been dictated by a crisis of conscience. It was rather a testimony to the depth of his understanding of the Christian message. In his preaching, he embodied an enthusiasm that revealed the ideals of his youth. His severity and moral rigorism have been mistaken for the rantings of a pitiless censor, too greatly influenced by the cynico-stoic style of the day. But in fact, while he does reflect the mannerisms of his times, the morality and spirituality he preached were well enmeshed in the concrete, everyday necessities of life in the world. His insistence on penance for

[42]PG 51, 235.
[43]PG 51, 214.

sin and compunction were well within the Christian tradition; and he broke with the Stoics in the final analysis of compassion and love for one's neighbor. In the end, he held up the monastic ideal of continual prayer, meditation, fasting, and alms-giving as an ideal buttressed by the imitation of Christ, and within the reach of all.

Chapter Six

The Western Fathers II

Hilary of Poitiers (315-367)

Born in Aquitania of a well-to-do family and educated in the rhetorical tradition, Hilary was converted to Christianity by his philosophical interests and a reading of the Scriptures. Though married, he was elected bishop of Poitiers by clergy and people; but was forced into exile in Phyrgia by the Arians. He used the opportunity to write his *On the Trinity* in twelve books that together with his treatise *On the Synods* proved a bridge between the theology of the oriental and the western Churches.

Hilary as exegete functions ordinarily more as moralist and director of souls, above all else pursuing edification so that in the severe though just God of the Old Testament, his preoccupation is to discover the good and merciful God of the New Testament.

In his three main exegetical works, the *Commentarium in S. Mattheum*, the *Tractatus super Psalmos*, and the *Tractatus Mysteriorum*, Hilary deals with the main problems raised by the Christian moral doctrine. Thus he discusses

man as made in the image of God which has been beclouded
by original sin, but given the possiblity of being refurbished
through the Redemption and divine grace which re-
established man's free will. For it is his *liberum arbitrium*
—free will — that is the secret of man's essential nobility.

> Through God's in-breathing Adam's living soul is acti-
> vated. He has received a law and is allowed free will
> whereby he is constituted independent of all worldly
> domination and made an inhabitant of paradise. Consi-
> dered worthy of the devil's envy, after his sin, he is
> preserved by God's mercy and is instructed in the knowl-
> edge of God in every age of this world. *Homily On
> Psalm* 14[1]

Hilary discusses the psychology of sin, and the salutary
effect of the confession of sins without contributing to the
solution of the problems raised by modern historians concerning ancient Christian practices. Finally, in the introduction to the *De Trinitate* he provides us with a consideration
of the process of conversion, employing what is almost
certainly a literary device and not a true history of his own
religious experience.

In his explanation of Psalm 14 — *Lord who will inhabit
your tabernacle* — Hilary proceeds to integrate the moral
requirements of both the Old and the New Testaments
without observing the *caesura* supplied by the advent of
Christ, and thus makes the moral obligations of both laws
co-equal. He considers this Psalm as a brief, practical precept which he says, with a bow to Cicero's *Pro Archia*, can
easily be memorized and serve one everywhere "at home and
abroad, publicly and privately, by day and by night." Since
it describes the man who walks without stain and achieves
justice — it is a summation of all that is required in prosecut-
ing the ascent toward God — the *iter ad Deum* — which will
eventuate in eternal rest. Despite its brevity, it is a distilla-

tion of the "rich and infinite precepts of the the Old and New Testaments proper for children as well as for men and (*in Psalm* 14.1) women." *Homily on Psalm* 14.1[2]

Hilary immediately proceeds to an allegorical interpretation of the verse, "who inhabits your tabernacle," by stating that the tents or huts which Moses instructed the chosen people to construct from the branches of trees to protect themselves against the elements were imaginary, and refer rather to the protection of the Law and the Gospel which those who would serve God must utilize in their journey toward eternity. In like manner Hilary describes "the mountain of the Lord" as Christ.

> Who has taken a body *ex homine* in which He now dwells above every principality and power ... and upon which mountain (namely, Christ) Has been built the city ... which is His body, the Church, whereunto those men belong who have been elected in His body before the constitution of the world. (*Homily on Psalm* 14.86)[3]

Immediately spelling out the significance of this event in the moral order, Hilary maintains that that man alone will inhabit the Lord's tent:

> Who enters uncontaminated and lives beyond every stain of sin ... and to whom, after the washing of baptism, no *sordes* or corruption adheres; but immaculate and resplendent, his body is not contaminated by impurities, nor his eyes demeaned by theatrical spectacles, nor his mind beclouded with wine, and whose life is not a slave to money. *Homily on Psalm* 14. 6[4]

[2]CSEL 22.
[3]CSEL 22, 86.
[4]CSEL 22, 88.

To do the work demanded by justice, good must not only be contemplated but achieved, benevolence must not merely be initiated but brought to completion, for justice only produces fruit when it is accomplished.

Yet even this does not suffice, for the Gentiles do these things by avoiding vice, that they may be of good repute. Distinguishing with St. Paul between the animal, the carnal, and the spiritual man, Hilary describes the carnal man as given to the services of the body with its concomitant vices. He credits the animal man with following his good instincts to accomplish what is *decens et honestum* —decent and honest— and by distinguishing between the *utilia* and *honesta* —useful and proper— in Stoic fashion, he spurns money, controls his appetites, avoids ambition, and thus becomes venerable in his goodness.

But the spiritual man acts in accordance with his knowledge of God, carrying out his Divine Will, pursuing God's secret counsels and the wisdom hidden from the world

> Which is knowable through revelation and the gift of the Holy Spirit, namely: the significance of God's having become incarnate, his triumph on the cross, and his exercising of power over death through the resurrection. *Homily on Psalm* 14.7[5]

Even here, however, evidently based on his personal experience in the battle over orthodoxy, Hilary has reservations. The truly spiritual man must achieve union with Christ who is absolute truth.

> "For many," he says, "fatigue their bodies by fasting, give testimony of their constancy by distributing their goods to the poor, and of their chasteness by practicing virginity," but unless their faith is adequate in accepting Christ in the fullness of his divinity, they are deficient. Not only

must they confess Christ as he is in himself, but they must conform to the requirements of truth in every day life. *Homily on Psalm* 14.8[6]

This, he admits, and he is apparently echoing Tertullian, is most difficult, since daily some type of mendacity seems unavoidable when, for example,

It is necessary not to betray one who is hiding against a persecutor, or give testimony for one in peril, or conceal the fatal illness from the sick. *Homily On Psalm* 14. 9-10[7]

Hilary would seem to justify such dissimulation covering it with St. Paul's advice that *"doctrinam nostram sale esse conditam"* (Col. 4:6) — our teaching must be tempered with salt.

He advises that there is a further step to be taken wherein a man who is innocent at heart, who pursues justice and truth, and does not deceive himself or others, must tend toward perfection. This requires the control, the rejection, and finally the destruction of a tendency common to all mankind, namely pride, with its temptation to domineer over others. Hilary terms this vice "the most inane of human qualities" for it destroys both the possibility of coming to penance oneself, and of truly influencing others. He further supplies a brief allusion to what modern moralists term "fraternal correction," suggesting that the proper means of helping others to see the light is not by bitterness and innuendo, but by the *blandimentum* of one's own *emendatio* — the gentleness of our own correction.

In rounding out his consideration of the moral life, Hilary insists that courage be joined to humility, whereby one can truly enjoy the liberty of the sons of God, facing evil and scandal without flinching, and not being intimidated by respect for persons.

[6]CSEL 22, 90.
[7]CSEL 22, 90-91.

On the existential plane, he considers the economic situation of his day, using the text supplied by the Psalm—*who does not give his money to usury*—to warn against usury, and along with a strong condemnation of this practice, he forbids the acceptance of emoluments or bribes on the part of judges and other officials, while suggesting that in accepting what is one's own due by way of payment or compensation for goods or services, a certain what we might term *noblesse oblige* is proper, again giving as motivation the perfect practice of charity.

From these observations it will be seen that, as a moralist, Hilary follows the tradition that goes back at least as far as Irenaeus, and grafts onto the Law of Christ those elements in the surrounding culture that justify reference to the moral teaching of the early Christian *paideia*. Throughout his *Commentary on the Psalms* his primary concern is to edify in the sense of supplying moral and ascetical direction for what he terms the "science of life" exercised under the guidance of Divine Wisdom incarnate in the world in the person of Christ, and extended through the ages in the Church. Functioning as one of the earlier bridges between the practical moralism of the west and the mystical theologizing of the oriental fathers, he manifests a clear and precise approach to the problems of daily life as they must be faced here and now, but *sub specie aeternitatis*. His anthropology is at once biblical and Stoic in orientation; his awareness of the world almost sociological in its comprehension; and there are many indications of a modification of his thought under the pressure of his personal experiences.

Ambrose of Milan (339-397)

Born in Trier of a notable Roman family, Ambrose received a legal education as a rhetorician and followed his father in a political career as an imperial official. While prefect of Liguria with headquarters in Milan, he was elected bishop by public acclamation. Baptized on November 24, 373, he was ordained a bishop on December 7. He disposed of the major portion of his wealth in favor of the Church and the poor reserving only a portion for support of his sister Marcellina, who had taken the veil as a nun.

Speaking of his task as a preacher, Ambrose confessed:

> It will be said, behold, he was not nourished in the bosom of the Church, nor was he disciplined from youth, but pulled from the tribunal and forced out of the vanities of this world, satisfied not with the call of the herald, but the song of the prophets. He remained in the priesthood not of his own power but by the grace of God. *On Penance* 2.78[8]

Nevetherless, Ambrose asserts:

> We could not escape the office of teaching which the requirement of the priesthood placed upon us despite our reluctance. *On Duties* 1,2[9]

Ambrose widened his pastoral knowledge with a reading of the Greek churchmen, particularly Philo Judaeus, Origen, Didymus, Cyril of Jerusalem, Basil and the two Gregories. In his tracts, sermons and scriptural commentaries, he covered almost every topic of Christian interest.

Augustine attests his effectiveness:

> I listened to him dispensing the word of truth to his people every Sunday. I was enraptured by his words and delighted by the beauty of his speech. *Conf.* 1.6.4[10]

As a theologian, Ambrose confesses that it was in consequence of his familiarity with the pagan moralists that he felt compelled to concentrate on Christian values. His treatise *On the Duty of Ministers* (De officiis ministrorum) *is a direct Christian adaptation of Cicero's De Officiis.*

[8]PL 16, 514-515.
[9]PL 16, 24.
[10]PL 32, 721.

On these matters certain students of philosophy have
written such as Paenetius and his followers among the
Greeks; Cicero among the Latins. I find this not distant
from our idea of duty compelling me to employ my pen.
As Cicero wrote for the education of his son, so I do for
the formation of my children. Nor do I love you whom I
engendered in the Gospel less than if I had begotten you
in marriage. Nature is not more vehement in loving than
is grace. For we should love more those with whom we
are to spend eternity than those with whom we are to be
only in this world. *On Duties* 24[11]

In this rather self-serving approach to brotherly love,
Ambrose indicates an essential feature of his moral teaching. Whereas the pagans strove for the good life — *beata
vita* — he raised his sights to eternal life — *vita eterna*. And
while discussing the various aspects of human interest from
a rational viewpoint, his thought is always dominated by the
revelation of the Word of God in the Scriptures. Thus in
considering the secular value involved in what is honest and
proper in human conduct, he immediately makes reference
to the Psalm 64 that begins; *Te decet Deus in Sion* (For you
O God, how proper (*decet*) is a Song in Sion). But instead of
the casuistic system of the pagans who distinguished
between what is honest on rational criteria and what is
useful in ethical judgments, Ambrose looks for the foundation of Christian morality in the will of God as elucidated in
the Scriptures.

For us there is nothing honest or useful unless we define it
as a grace for eternal life and not what is aimed at for
enjoyment here. Hence our understanding is not superfi-
cial since we judge our duty by a different standard than
what they use. For they take the convenient things of this
world as good. But we see these things as possibly a

[11]PL 16, 30.

detriment. He who received good things here as did Dives may be penalized hereafter. *On Duties* 28[12]

As a foundation of his moral thinking, Ambrose postulates a supernatural order. Paraphrasing Cicero, he begins:

There is nothing in which man surpasses the animal world more than in his participation in reason and his seeking out the causes of things. *On Duties* 124[13]

Accepting the classic Stoic pattern of upright living, Ambrose discusses the Christian life under the four classic virtues of prudence, justice, fortitude and temperance. In the *De Officiis*, Ambrose had begun with a consideration of the virtue of *pietas* — respect for one's forebears. He changed its objective from the human to the divine. He thus re-ordered the ethics of humanism. For the Christian, piety is the reverence for God the Creator, and not merely a habit of self-realization or adjustment to social demands based on family and patriotism that was the source of duty and the criterion of conduct among the good pagans. In turn, Ambrose's concept of *pietas* required a recognition of the part played by divine grace in the conduct of believers.

An assiduous preacher, Ambrose covered the whole of the Old Testament with his commentaries, beginning with the *Hexaemeron* in which he followed both Philo and Basil the Great. He wrote on *Cain and Abel*, *On Noah and the Ark, Isaac and the Soul, Jacob and Flight from the World, Joseph the Patriarch*, a commentary on the *Gospel of Luke*, and he gave considerable attention to the state of virginity as well as widowhood.

To his own amazement, Ambrose became the great champion of virginity. In an age in which women were almost totally subject to their husband's legal as well as familial domination, the Church's stress on virginity became a great

[12]PL 16, 32.
[13]PL 16, 60.

liberation movement particularly for women of the upper classes and of means. Ambrose reflects on the effectiveness of his preaching in a codex of sermons he gathered:

> Someone says you sing the praises of virginity to us daily. What am I to do who sing these praises daily here and accomplish nothing? But obviously it is not my fault. For virgins come here from Placentina to be blessed; they come here from Bononia; they come from Mauritania that they may take the veil here. You see a great happening. I preach here; and I persuade in other localities. If this is the case, I will perform in other places that I may persuade you here. *On Virgins* 1.57[14]

Conscious of the needs of the majority of his flock, Ambrose observes at the same time:

> Nor did I dissuade from matrimony even while I built up the benefits of virginity. *On Virgins* 1.24[15]

In dealing with marriage, Ambrose insists on its sacred character:

> Nor do we deny that marriage has been sanctified by Christ whose divine voice said, "They will be two in one flesh" (Matthew 19.3) "and in one spirit . . . . " It is right that an upright wife is to be praised, but it is even better when a pious virgin receives preference. *Epistle* 42.3[16]

But where Cicero proceeds to praise the investigation of the natural sciences, Ambrose contends:

> Man realizes that he has to search out the author of life in whose power is the control of our life and death; who rules this world by his will; to whom we know we have to

[14]PL 16, 204-205.
[15]PL 16, 195.
[16]PL 16, 1124.

render an account of our actions. There is nothing that so adds to an honest life than that we believe him to be our future judge from whom occult things are not hidden and whom bad deeds offend and good things delight. *Ibid.* 1.24[17]

On this background he describes human relationships that give rise to moral values:

To no one is it allowed to know (carnally) a woman other than his wife. Hence, the right of marriage is given to you lest you fall into a trap and do evil with another woman. (Paul cautions) *You are bound to a woman; do not seek a divorce* (1 Cor. 7.27) for it is not licit for you while your wife lives to marry another woman. For to seek another when you have your own is the crime of adultery, and this becomes the more grave when you consider using the authority of the law to cover your sin. *On Abraham* 1.7.59[18]

On the matter of the forgiveness of sins, Ambrose proves astute in his brief observations.

It is evident from the Lord's preaching that there is a mandate for those guilty of even the most grave crimes— if they do penance from the bottom of the heart together with an open confession of their sin, grace will be afforded them in this heavenly sacrament. *On Penance* 2.3.19[19]

If you wish to be justified, confess your sin. A sorrowful confession of sins dissolves the binding of crimes. Look at what God demands of you that you be mindful of his grace and do not carry on as if you had not received it. See

[17]PL 16, 60.
[18]PL 14, 442.
[19]PL 16, 501.

with what solicitude of forgiveness he provokes you to confession. *Ibid.* 2.6.40-41[20]

As a moralist, Ambrose proved a stable guide to the development of the Christian ethic and way of life with an influence that reached down the ages.

Rufinus of Aquileia (345-410)

It would be of considerable interest had we a testament concerning the precise moral teachings of Rufinus of Aquileia similar to the dogmatic statements contained in his *Apologia against Jerome*, his *Apologia to Pope Anastasius*, and developed at some length in his *Commentary on the Apostles' Creed*. Instead, for a rounded picture of his moral doctrine we have to turn to his translations of Origen's works, to two treatises of St. Basil — eight homilies selected from among the Cappadocian doctor's moral discourses, and an adaptation of Basil's *Monastic Rules* — and to Rufinus' own *De Benedictionibus Patriarcharum*.

Through his experiences as a monastic founder in Jerusalem, as well as his interests in spreading the fruits of eastern asceticism among the select souls he encountered on his return to the West in 397, Rufinus was conscious of the necessity of a definite moral training for those dedicated to the Christian way of life. This is made apparent in his preface to his translation of nine *Homilies of Origen on the Psalms* which he undertook for the convert layman Apronianus in 398. Distinguishing carefully between the moral and the ascetical approach, Rufinus explains his reason for choosing this particular work of Origen:

> These Homilies offer certain precepts for an emended way of life, and teach first the way of penance and conversion, then that of purgation and progress. *Origen's Homilies on Psalms 36-38, Preface*[21]

[20]PL 16, 507.
[21]CCL 20, 251.

He is anxious that such ideas should likewise be placed before religiously minded women to provide them with a clear and simple treatment of the Christian way of life. He assures Apronianus' spouse Avita that such reading "will afford her benefit .... "

> Indeed a simplicity of life is here taught by easy discourse in lucid terms, whence its portent (*prophetia*) can be applied not alone to men, but also to religious women .... He further remarks that even in matters of mortality a gentle approach is proper since "not even the human body can be all sinews and bones, God in his providence having fitted it with the softness of flesh and a comfortable plumpness (*blandimenta pinguedinis*)." *Ibid.*

In the preface with which he introduced the *Homilies of St. Basil*, again addressed to Apronianus sometime in 400 or 401, Rufinus writes, apparently from Aquileia:

> You once requested, my dear Apronianus, that I translate something into Latin for you. This I have already done in part while with you in Rome. Now I have added something more; for I have translated these eight short sermons by the blessed Basil.

> His work is thus more moral in nature, fit for guiding souls toward the good life and for relieving them in their labors. In this also it possesses greater virtue in that its perusal will be found most suitable for religiously minded women, and particularly for the admiring study of our matronly daughter, since it is not burdened with questions of a dogmatic nature, but rather it goes along as a most limpid stream, flowing softly and with sufficient calm. *Preface to Homilies of Basil*[22]

In consequence of his own experiences as a monastic leader in Jerusalem over the course of almost twenty years,

---

[22]CCL 20, 237.

as well as of his familiarity with the Desert Fathers, Rufinus had decided to adapt and translate the *Rules of St. Basil* for Abbot Ursacius with whom he had spent the Lent of 398 in the monastery at Pinetum near Terracina.

> Since you were taken with his ideas and opinions, you eagerly demanded that I translate this work into Latin, promising me that if throughout the monasteries of the West, they should come to know these sacred and spiritual rules of this spiritual and saintly man, every advance of the servants of God which might be begotten of these institutes would be for me, through their merits and prayers, a token of grace and mercy. *Preface to Basil's Rules*[23]

What is immediately noticeable about this "rule" is its attention to the moral problems that are fundamental to the Christian way of life. The questions deal with the nature and possibility of the practice of continence; with particular virtues such as meekness, obedience, poverty, temperance, fraternal charity, the cause and cure for evil thoughts and bad dreams, the obligation to forgive slights on the part of the brethren, as well as the method of dealing with deliquent practitioners of the rules and admonitions. And the scriptural quotations introduced to buttress the argument, unlike a good deal of the Alexandrian typological and allegorical method, are immediately pertinent and apt.

Thus, for example, in dealing with the possibility of restraining one's anger, the answer is given to the question: "How does one keep from growing angry?"

> If one believes that God sees all things and the Lord is acknowledged as always present. For no one who is subject to a judge will dare to manifest any of his indignation in the presence of his judge. Likewise, if he does not consider others as subject to himself, but prepare himself

> for obedience to others .... If one is not seeking the
> obedience of others for his own benefit ... when he sees
> them break the law of God he will not be moved with
> anger, but rather with compassion and mercy following
> St. Paul's "Who is weak, and I am not weak?" (2 Corin-
> thians 11:29) Shorter Rules, *Interrogation* XXIX[24]

In general these answers seize upon the various statements and admonitions found in the Gospels concerning the
practice of virtue and the avoidance of vice. The basis for the
doctrine advanced is laid down particularly in questions
eight and nine having to do with the nature and the practice
of continence under which term the whole discipline of the
virtuous life is summarized:

> That I may put it briefly, all things that are sought after
> through mortal concupiscence — to abstain from these
> things, this is the virtue of continence. Hence it is not only
> in the eating of food or in the libido that the virtue of
> continence is acknowledged; but when we abstain from
> all things wherein the flesh has pleasure, but in which the
> soul is wounded. Likewise the truly continent does not
> seek earthly glory; but he holds himself back from vices
> — from wrath, and from sorrowfulness and from all
> those things which commonly keep uninstructed and
> incautious souls occupied. *Interrogation* XVI[25]

It is this Basilian spirit that underlies the moral teaching
of the *De Benedictionibus Patriarcharum—On the Blessings at the Patriarchs*—which Rufinus wrote at the request
of Paulinus of Nola, probably in 408. The method of scriptural exegesis is strictly patterned on Origen, utilizing the
allegorical and typological interpretation for discussing the
historical, the mystical, and the moral meaning of individual words and passages. Rufinus confesses:

[24]PG 31, 1101.
[25]PG 31, 960.

> Sacred Scripture should not only contain a knowledge of
> the mysteries, but it should likewise inform the morals
> and the activities of the one learning ...   Hence we have
> endeavored, after having described in as far as we are
> able, these two meanings — that is according to the
> historical and the mystical sense — to discuss the moral
> meaning contained therein. We desire that the readers
> should learn not only what was done for and by others,
> but what they themselves should do for themselves.
> *On the Blessings* 1, 11[26]

In this treatise Rufinus summarizes the basic motivation
behind the Christian's moral way of life. He contends with
St. Paul that the faithful, redeemed in the Church through
the blood of Christ, are members of Christ's body once they
have been regenerated by the grace of baptism. He insists,
however, that a knowledge of God and an awareness of their
position in the mystical body is not sufficient. Rather are
they as:

> The feet of Christ to function by running to make peace,
> and by hastening to help those in necessity. Serving as the
> hands of Christ, they are to extend mercy, giving aid to
> the indigent, and proffering assistance to the sick. They
> will be the eyes of Christ when they show forth the light
> (of faith) before the whole world. *On the Blessings* 1, 10[27]

Turning to the psychological constitution of the human
person, Rufinus reminds his readers that:

> there is a natural law within us which accuses everyone
> who sins; and reminds him that the sin he commits is evil.
> *On the Blessings* 2,6[28]

[26]CCL 20, 199.
[27]CCL 20, 198.
[28]CCL 20, 207.

He then traces the source of sin to three inclinations: anger, cupidity and unreasoning—the irascible, concupiscible and rational appetites. This analysis he says is the traditional one handed down from of old.

By grace, however, a man can repent of his evil doings, be converted to the right road of virtue, and desire the good, even while he finds himself still in the midst of a fateful world. The Christian, Rufinus insists, should look upon fate (*sors*) not with the gentiles as something that happens by pure chance. Rather it is:

> the portion of one's inheritance which is given to each one ... by the judgment and dispensation of God. The fates are thus to be understood by us in this moral exposition as the commandments of God through which is obtained our heavenly inheritance. He therefore who is once converted, and now seeks the wages of his labors, is always in the midst of his fate—that is, in the midst of God's commandments. *Ibid.*[29]

The Christian can turn himself from the works of darkness by controlling his thoughts and turning them to the things of eternity. Comforting himself as God's farmer, before whom God holds out both rest and the earth which is good, he must purge his flesh of its vices and concupiscences, and bring forth the fruit of justice by his good works. Thus he proceeds as God's good farmer,

> ceaselessly cultivating the field of his mind and the meadow-land (*novalia*) of his heart with the plough-share of God's word and the blade of the Scriptures. He waters the plants of faith and charity, of hope and justice from the fountains of Israel and adapts the whole discipline of agriculture in the field of his mind. *Ibid.*[30]

[29]CCL 20, 212.
[30]CCL 20, 213.

Following each of the historical and mystical explana-
tions of these twelve prophecies or benedictions, Rufinus
gives an array of enlightening counsels for the moral way of
life. He speaks of the necessity of acknowledging one's sins;
he describes the reaches of humility; he warns of the need for
fidelity to his own message expected in the one preaching
the Gospel. Finally, he refers to an idea he had already
expressed in his preface to the *Homilies of St. Basil*: the true
Christian has to "accept a martyrdom of the conscience,
which unceasingly he must bear within himself."

St. Jerome (347-420)

Even in the most charitable evaluation, Jerome of
Stridon was an irascible churchman. He did his classical
studies in Rome and, after a somewhat misspent youth, was
baptized and joined an ascetic community in Aquileia
before spending two years in the Syrian desert as a hermit.
After a *Wanderjahr* in palestine and Egypt, he became
secretary to Pope Damasus. Retiring to Bethlehem, he
founded a double monastery where as a man of three languages — Hebrew, Greek and Latin— he became the most
renowned of the Church's scripture scholars. As with most
misogynists, Jerome's career was dominated by pious
women from his aunt, Castoriana, to the well-to-do
matrons — Paula and Eustochium, Blessilla and Marcella
— of the Aventine hill in Rome. His scriptural expertise,
caustic pen and irascible temperament made him one of the
most formidable champions of orthodoxy in the early
Church.

As a moralist Jerome reflects both the Stoic mores and
the Christian idealism that criss-crossed each other in the
early Church. The better part of his ethical teaching is in his
letters and scripture commentaries. In his polemical tracts
against Jovinian, Helvidius and Pelagius, his mordant pen
frequently betrays the grave exaggerations of the satirist
doing an injustice to the subject in hand. At his best, Jerome
is a colorful observer of the virtues and vices of contempor-

ary society; at his worst, he is a combative polemicist intent on destroying opponents in the conviction that he alone possessed a monopoly on revealed truth.

Scattered through his voluminous scripture commentaries, his letters, polemical treatises and learned tracts are innumerable observations on the moral exigencies of the Christian way of life. He tells mothers how to educate their children in the Lord, particularly girls who are to be consecrated as virgins. He excoriates with glee the aberrations of priests and clerics cultivating the rich and powerful; and he discusses the intimate relationship between grace, the temptation of the soul as well as the flesh, and the possibility of living an integral Christian life. In the long run, he furnishes no constructive treatise on the Christian ethic; nevertheless, his innumerable observations on human conduct in the light of the Gospel furnished the Church down the ages with a fount of wisdom and moral reflection.

As a foundation for his moral commitment, Jerome asserts:

> The study of piety is to know the law, to understand the prophets, to believe in the Gospels and not to ignore the Apostles. While, on the one hand, there are many who have a good grasp of piety, they do not have a knowledge of the arts or other truths. *Commentary on Epistle to Titus*, 1.2[31]

In his Scripture commentaries, Jerome fleshes out an anthropology that combines an allegorical interpretation of the Jewish prophets with his own classical formation. He insists that mankind's creation in the image of God, refers to the soul and not to the body.

On the principal passions, Jerome asserts:

> We read in Plato that it is a common teaching among philosophers that there are three passions in the human

soul: the *logicon* that we can interpret as reason; the *thumikon* that we call wrath or irascible; and the *epithumikon* or the appetite of the concupiscence. Philosophers locate our reason in the brain; wrath in the spleen, and desire in the liver. *Commentary on Matthew Book* 2.13:33[32]

Jerome takes note of the function of conscience:

Above reason and the appetites of concupiscence and wrath there is a fourth element which the Greeks call syneidesis. It is the spark of conscience which even in the breast of Cain, after he was ejected from paradise, was not extinguished. It is that by which after being overcome by pleasure, or wrath, or the deceptions of our reason, we still know that we have sinned. *Commentary on Ezechial*, 1.6[33]

Following Paul's *Epistle to Titus*, Jerome outlines the structure of Christian morality for the four classes of the faithful: senior men, and women, young men, and young ladies.

Now he explains what is becoming to each age. And first he spells out what is proper to older men, then what is becoming to older women; thirdly what is correct for youth, both male and female, although in his precepts for older women he puts forth the rules for younger women, so that it is not so much he who is teaching the younger ones as explaining what they are to be taught by their elders. Finally, he sets up precepts proper for servants in each age and condition so that his discourse is a rule of life and morals.

Older men are to be sober or vigilant, for the Greek *nephoalios* has both meanings; be honest that the gravity

[32]PL 26, 91.
[33]CCL 75-12.

of age may adorn the gravity of behavior; chaste, lest they luxuriate in an age foreign to them and with blood cold to passion they set an example leading youth to ruin. They should be sane not only in faith but in charity, and in patience ... who indeed possesses the sanity of charity, unless he who first loves God with the whole mind. *Commentary on Titus*, 2.2[34]

Commenting on Paul's complaint that older women are frequently garrulous, Jerome says,

And certainly because they have overpassed their youth, they dispute about the ages of younger women, and say; "This one so dresses," "that one thus combs her hair," "that other one walks so," "she loves this one," "she is loved by someone else."

Even though these accusations be true, they should not be ventilated before others, but corrected secretly with the charity of Christ. They should be taught not to do such things rather than publicly accused of what they have done. These ages are accustomed to give themselves to wine for lust; and between cups, they see themselves as prudent but talkative, assuming a certain anxiety of morals, speaking out about what they think and not remembering what they were. Hence, older women should be forbidden from taking too much wine since what in youth is bad in old age becomes drunkenness. *Commentary on Titus*, 2.3[35]

Jerome comments on married women:

(Paul) desires them to love their husbands chastely and desires a chaste affection to prevail between husband and wife so that with modesty and reverence, as it were, she

[34]PL 26, 578.
[35]PL 26, 580.

accepts the necessity of sex that she renders her spouse rather than ask it of him; and she recognizes that she is then engaged in the begetting of children before the eyes of angels and of God. *Commentary on Titus*[36]

Further commenting on St. Paul's admonition that a woman should fear her husband, Jerome indulges a certain irony:

If the fear of God because of punishment prevents the one so fearing from being perfect, how much more imperfect is the woman who fears both God and her husband? Hence, it must be asked whether the wife is here thought of carnally under the guise of fear. Frequently wives are found to be much better than their husbands, guiding them, governing the household, educating the children, and presiding over the family discipline, while their men run after luxurious and impure pleasures. Whether these women should rule their husbands or fear them, I leave to the judgment of the reader! *Commentary on Ephesians* 3, 5,31[37]

In his confutation of Jovinian, Jerome states his fundamental attitude toward marriage:

Now since heretics have spurned marriage and condemned God's creation, we gladly listen to what is said in praise of marriage. For the Church does not condemn marriage, but governs it; it does not reject but dispenses it; knowing, as we said above, that in a great house there are not only vessels of gold and silver, but of wood and earth. *Adv. Jovinian I.*40[38]

[36]PL 26, 581.
[37]PL 26, 536.
[38]PL 23, 269-270.

Delving deeper into the problems presented by the sin of the first parents, which he equates with their sexual indulgences, Jerome suggests:

> Let us read the beginning of Genesis and we will find that Adam is designated as mankind, that is, as man and woman. Since then we were created good and righteous by God we have descended to evil by our will. What was righteous in us in Paradise has been depraved on our departure from Paradise. Now you can object that, before they sinned, the sex of the man and woman was differentiated, and that they were able to unite without sin. What might have been is unknown. Nor are we able to know the judgment of God or prejudge his sentence on our free will.
>
> What happened is apparent. They who were continent in Paradise, on being thrust from Paradise, copulated. They are expelled from Paradise; and what they did not do there they did on earth, so that from the start of the human condition Paradise was given to virginity and the earth to marriage. *Adv. Jovianian* 1.29[39]

For all his misogynism, Jerome insists that in God's sight there is equality between men and women.

> Caesar's laws are one thing, Christ's another; Papinian prescribes one thing, our Paul another. Among the pagans the restraints of chastity are relaxed for men and, while they condemn seduction and adultery, their libido is tolerated in brothels and prostitutes; as if dignity and not lust caused the fault. But among us what is not allowed to women is equally not for men and each is bound and judged by the same condition. *Epistle* 77[40]

[39]PL 23, 251.
[40]CSEL 55, 39.

In his commentary on Ecclesiastes, Jerome concedes:

> Moreover, since the human mind cannot gaze continu-
> ally toward the sublime, nor always contemplate higher
> and divine things, nor always be in contact with celestial
> matters, but at times must indulge the needs of the
> body—so there is a time for embracing wisdom and
> binding oneself to it more strictly; and there is a time for
> relaxing the mind from its contemplation of wisdom, for
> the care of the body and of those things that our life
> demands without sin. *Chapter 3*[41]

Commenting on Paul's "Let all bitterness and furor and
wrath and outcry and blasphemy be done away with along
with all malice," Jerome asserts:

> Bitterness is opposed to sweetness whence commonly
> people are called bitter or sweet ...   Furor is incipient
> wrath and indignation festering in the mind. Wrath, of
> which bitterness and furor are species, is that which
> desires revenge when furor is restrained and wishes to
> harm him whom it thinks had done harm. When we speak
> of the wrath of God ... such a movement of the mind is
> not to be thought of in the same fashion as it is in us. For
> when we grow wrathful, are perturbed and rapt in fury,
> we cease to be ourselves. Hence all bitterness, furor and
> wrath must be totally taken from us....
>   If wrath desires revenge—revenge wants to expend the
> evil it believes it has received on the one by whom it thinks
> itself injured—and this a Christian must not do since he is
> not to return evil for evil (cf. Romans 12.19). *Commen-
> tary on Ephesians* 3.31[42]

Despite his contentious approach to vice and virtue,
Jerome displays a great deal of sense in many of his apparently incidental observations. In a sudden fit of humility,

[41]PL 23, 1036.
[42]PL 23, 516.

dealing with a difficult sentence in the *Epistle to the Romans*, Jerome admits:

> It is much better simply to confess one's ignorance and, among the things we do not know, to take refuge in the obscurity of this passage. *Epistle* 120[43]

Likewise, he reflects a fundamental gentleness:

> While we live in the tabernacle of this body and are surrounded with this feeble flesh, we strive to moderate and control our passions and affections. We cannot amputate them! Hence, the Psalmist says, "Be angry and sin not" (4.5) and the Apostle (Paul) commenting urges, "Let not the sun go down on your anger." (Ephesians 4.26) To be angry is human; to put an end to anger, Christian. *Epistle* 130.13[44]

Finally, he maintains:

> I think it superfluous to remind you against avarice, since it is your kind to have and tread on riches. The Apostle teaches that avarice is the cult of idols (Ephesians 5.3). It is an apostolic ambition and perfect virtue to sell all and give it to the poor, and, thus unburdened and light, to fly with Christ to heaven. *Epistle* 130.14[45]

In view of this goal, Jerome suggests:

> In all ages and to everyone there is free will. "If you wish, be perfect. I do not force you, nor comment, nor even propose this victory. I merely hold up the reward."

---

[43]CSEL 55, 500.
[44]CSEL 56, 13.
[45]*Ibid.* 206.

Augustine of Hippo (345-430)

Augustine of Hippo is, if not the greatest, at least the most influential of the early church fathers. Born a Christian in Tagaste, North Africa, he was educated as a rhetorician and became an outstanding teacher obtaining a prestigious position in Milan. After a youth spent in physical debauchery and a period of intellectual wandering, he was converted to the Catholic faith. A prodigious writer, traveller and polemicist, he was selected Bishop of Hippo in his native province of Carthage and at once played an important part in the development of church teaching in both doctrinal and moral spheres. His *City of God* and his *Confessions* are classic Christian treatises. His innumerable homilies, tracts and letters cover the whole diapason of human interest in the fifth-century western church.

Speculation of modern critics to the effect that Augustine was converted to Neoplatonism rather than to the Christian faith are refuted by his own testimony. In his *Confessions* he says he gradually grew disenchanted with the pagan philosophy and sought the profundity and certainty of the Christian theology. Likewise in his *Retractations*, a series of "second-thoughts" about his earlier writings, he corrected many of the opinions he held before his baptism in such treatises as *On Order*, *On the Blessed Life*, etc.

In his experience of the self as a substantial acting person, Augustine finds the basis for his value system and responsibility. The human being, he maintains, does know certain things infallibly. It is beyond question that I exist, and know and love that existence. Even if I were mistaken, I am . . . .

Augustine discovered the nature of the human person in three functions:

> I desire that men consider these three things: I am, I know, and I will. I am one knowing and willing; I know myself to be and to will. I will to be and to know. In these three, then, let everyone who is able discern how inseparable life is in being one, with one mind and one essence —how inseparable a distinction, and yet a distinction.

We both exist and know that we exist; and all rejoice in this existence and this knowledge. In these three, then, when the mind knows itself and loves itself, there is a trinity of mind, love and knowledge. *Confessions* 13.11.12[46]

Applying this knowledge of the human self to its source in the Trinity, Augustine discovered a way to represent the uncreated Creator as a triune God in keeping with the evidence of the scriptures. This intuition, he claimed, was not achieved by reasoning, but by faith. Where the mystic philosopher Plotinus found ecstasy in the contemplation of the divinity as One, Augustine finds total satisfaction in discovering God as three persons. "From God," he maintains, "we derive the beginning of existence, the principle of knowledge and the law of affection" (*Contra Faustum*).

Augustine traces the nature of sin and error to a bad will rooted in a bad love.

As a slave to sin the man who knows what is good and fails to do it eventually loses the power to know what is good. If a man having power to do what is right is unwilling, he then loses power to do what he wills. *On Free Will* 3

Augustine's view of evil contrasts with that of the Greek theologians, particularly Gregory of Nyssa. The latter concentrates on the demonic structure of evil that assumes an integral place in the Christian scheme of reality. Not only does Gregory recognize sin as registered in man's conscience, but he acknowledges the existence of evil prior to man's fall in which mankind is seduced through deception by the devil. (cf. Gregory of Nyssa, *On Virginity,* 12[47])

Augustine, on the other hand, does not pose the question, "What is evil?" Rather, he asks, "When do we commit evil?"

[46]PL 32, 849; CCL 27, 247-248.
[47]PG 46, 369.

In his *On Order, On Free Will* and in his *Confessions*, he explains that evil arises from the fact that the soul turns to lesser goods rather than to the highest good. Hence, the defect that is evil is brought about by the human person through his own fault. The devil, then, is only an instrument in God's hands who carries out a divine judgment on sinful men and women.

Augustine denies any basic break between the life of thought and that of the senses:

> From the soul and from the body that are parts of man we arrive at the totality which is man. Thus, the life of the soul is not one thing, and that of the body another. Rather the two are one and the same — that is, the life of the human being as human being. *City of God* 14.4[48]

By insisting that the passions and emotions are an integral part of the individual person, Augustine avoids the error of considering the human being as essentially a spiritual entity imprisoned in a body. He goes on to insist:

> Every living soul, and not only the rational or human soul, but also the irrational souls of cattle, birds and fish, is moved by representations of things perceived. But while irrational beings are immediately moved by these representations so that they are impelled to act in accord with their nature, the rational soul is at liberty to consent or withhold consent from these representations. *On Genesis* 9:14-25[49]

In its activities, human reason thus functions in three stages: *suggestion* that arises from thought or sense-perception; *cupidity* or a natural desire to enjoy what is perceived; and the *consent* or the *refusal* of the reason.

---

[48]CSEL 40, 2.9.
[49]PL 34, 402.

This freedom to choose is attributed to free will which Augustine defines as the "uncoerced motion of the mind, making the attainment of an object or its rejection."

There is nothing I feel with such solid intimate assurance as that I have a will, and that it is by this will that I am moved to all forms of satisfaction. Will is certainly in all mankind; nay, we are nothing else but wills. For what are desire and pleasure other than will in consenting to those things that we want? And what are fear and distress other than will in dissenting from those things that we do not want? *On Free Will, Bk.* 3, 3.12[50]

By insisting so absolutely on the substantial nature of the will as the source of human individuality, Augustine rejected both the Platonist and the Manichean attempt to separate soul from body and thus divorce the passions of desire, fear, joy and pain from mankind's integral experience. He thereby establishes the source of sinfulness, not in the body, but in the soul where he locates the consciousness of the self and the faculties of reason and will, two different aspects of the soul.

In insisting that mankind enjoys fredom of the will, Augustine does not exclude determination through factors that may condition, but in no sense dictate, the final decision of the will. He acknowledges the effects of temperament, experience, education and ignorance. In the end, he distinguishes between what he calls a good will and a bad will and concludes that mankind has two choices: the two loves that built two cities — the good love centered on the City of God and the bad love concerned with the earthly city.

He describes the bad love as directed toward "the will to power" wherein he says:

The soul loving its own power, descends from the desire for the common and universal good to one which is

[50]CCL 29, 276.

> individual and private, and having achieved that pride
> that is called the foundation of sin. *On the Trinity*[51]

These individual goods can be a function of curiosity, or a
thirst to dominate, or more simply the "filthy whirl of
sensual pleasure," all of which involves a *cupiditas mundi* —
a cupidity for the world — the subordination of spiritual to
material goods. It is thus traced back to pride, the desire to
exercise one's power and so to "become like gods." In this
endeavor, there is a disregard for the fact that human nature
cannot achieve happiness in any real sense without
acknowledging the principle of its life and being — without,
in other words, accepting Augustine's final conclusion
regarding mankind's need for God: "Our hearts were made
for you; and will not rest until they rest in you!"

On the question of human conduct, Augustine early on
had adopted a pessimistic stance. Whether it was the direct
result of his own libidinous experiences as a young man and
the hangover from his Manichean attachments before his
conversion, Augustine's notion of the effects of original sin
borders on the drastic. The imperfection of mankind was a
profound and permanent dislocation. For Pelagius the decision to choose good and avoid evil was simply a matter of
self-control. For Augustine, the "desires of sin" were so
deeply rooted in human nature that they required a healing
that could only take place by means of a transfusion of grace
and the enabling assistance of the Holy Spirit.

> For we assert that the human will is so far assisted by
> divine aid that in the accomplishment of justice, over and
> above the fact that man is created with the power of
> voluntary self-determination, over and above the teach-
> ing whereby he derives precepts by which to live, he also
> receives the Holy Spirit whence is begotten in his mind
> the love for and delight in the supreme immortal good
> which is God, a free gift. *On the Spirit and the Letter* 3 [52]

[51]CCL 50, 368.
[52]PL 44, 203.

In his vivid description of the effects of original sin, Augustine has difficulty in avoiding appearing as a Manichean or extreme Platonist. He emphasizes the psychological tensions that are caused by the passions leading to loss of control of the sexual faculty, shame and the imagination. The life of the senses is not evil in itself. It is only the tension when the will directed by reason clashed with the appetites that led to evil. For Augustine, the one passion that inevitably and permanently clashed with reason was sexual desire.

In dealing with the particulars of moral life, Augustine experienced a considerable development not necessarily for the best in his teaching regarding sex and marriage. In his earlier consideration *On the Goodness of Marriage* (*De bono coniugali*), Augustine had suggested that the quality of sexual intercourse could be sanctified by the friendship of the two people in marriage:

> The good of marriage, therefore, it seems to me, is not only in the procreation of children, but also in the very natural society of the two partners. Otherwise there would be no marriage among the aged, particularly if they had lost their children, or never had any. *On the Goodness of Marriage* 3.3 [53]

> This happens because in that whereby the couple render their debt to one another, even if this involves some intemperance and incontinence, they owe fidelity to each other mutually. To this fidelity, the Apostle attributes so much of the law that he calls it power. The breaking of this fidelity is called adultery. *Ibid.*[54]

Later he took a more pessimistic attitude intimating that marital relations even with the intentions of procreating offspring could hardly ever be indulged without passion causing at least venial sin. He felt the effect of original sin

[53]CSEL 41, 190.
[54]CSEL 41, 191.

was so strong as to all but destroy the married person's moral integrity.

Augustine's most effective critic was the Pelagian bishop, Julian of Eclanum, who accused the Bishop of Hippo of holding "that there is a sin that is part of human nature." Julian rejects this contention by stating that such a teaching:

> "is unjust and impious; it makes it seem as if the devil were the maker of men. It violates and destroys the freedom of the will by saying that mankind is incapable of virtue because in the very womb of their mothers they are filled with bygone sins ... forcing on man throughout his life every form of wickedness." *Opus imperfectum* 3, 67[55]

In refuting Julian's contention, Augustine appealed to psychological and human experience. Sexual feeling as now experienced, he held, is obviously a penalty for former disobedience. In itself it is a torture of the will. As a permanent experience it manifests itself in the imagination, in dreams and in "a pressing throng of desires."

> We have in us evil desires, by not consenting to which, we do not live badly. There is in us the concupiscence of sins; by not obeying, we do not do evil; but by having them, we do not achieve good. The Apostle demonstrates that good is not achieved here when such concupiscence is not obeyed. *On Marriage and Concupiscence* 1.24.27[56]

In the overall consideration, Augustine's moral thinking was permeated with the conviction that life here was merely a preparation for the next world. Hence, worldly pleasures were a distraction. This conviction he hammered home most vividly in his consideration of sexual pleasures and the legitimacy of marriage. There is no doubt, however, that his teaching on original sin and the nature of concupiscence

[55]PL 45, 1278-1279.
[56]PL 44, 429.

were fundamentally influenced by his experiences as a lascivious youth and his early adherence to the Manichean sect.

In the long run, Augustine concludes:

> Two loves, therefore, have made two cities. There is an earthly city made by the love of self even to the point of contempt for God; and a heavenly city made by the love of God even to contempt of self. The earthly city takes great pride in self, while the celestial city glories in God. The terrestial city looks for glory among men. But our conscience gives witness that God is the greatest glory in the heavenly city. *The City of God* 14.28[57]

Pope Leo I (440-461)

Pope Leo the Great was doubtlessly the finest mind and most efficient of all the early Bishops of Rome. As a deacon under Pope Celestine, he had prepared a syllabus on grace that incorporated traditional church teaching in refuting the heresy of Pelagianism. He had also persuaded John Cassian to assemble a similar treatise on the Incarnation. As pope, he proved to be a great preacher and pastoral letter-writer, who discussed the problems affecting the local and the universal Church in a realistic fashion. On accepting the papacy to which he was elected while on a long journey, Leo acknowledged the universal priesthood of the laity presided over by Christ with the pope as Bishop of Rome acting in the place of Peter *cuius vice fungimur* — in whose stead we function.

As Bishop of Rome, Leo dedicated himself to the priestly duty of preaching. A representative selection of his sermons for the whole liturgical cycle have been preserved: 10 for Christmas, 8 for Epiphany, 12 for Lent, 19 on the Passion,

[57]CSEL 40.2, 56.

2 for Easter, 2 for the Ascension, 3 for Pentecost, one for the Feast of St. Peter and another for St. Lawrence, 23 for the Ember days, which he says are celebrated four times in the year (Sermon 19.2) when the faithful fast on Wednesday, Friday and Saturday and then celebrate the vigil of Sunday at St. Peter's.

Six sermons describe the distribution of alms to the poor as of apostolic institution and to offset pagan superstitions. They advise the almsgiver to be aware of the poor who do not come forward out of shame or modesty. A sermon on Rome's deliverance, apparently from Gaiseric in 455, testifies to the survivance of astrology, the circus and pagan spectacles (Sermon 84). Leo reproved the custom of bowing toward the sun and condemned as *paganitatis spiritu* (in the spirit of paganism) the notion that December 25 marks the rise of the New Sun rather than the birth of Christ (Sermon 27.4).

In his homilies he describes the spiritual life of the faithful, stressing their involvement in the struggle for sanctity. Leo's vocabulary and style manifest a total accomodation of the Christian message to the Latin culture of which he is a perfect master. Though a Roman of the Romans, he lived a life in immediate contact with Christ and the apostles:

> We see what they saw, touch what they touched. Not in history alone do we perceive these things; but in virtue of their current enactments.

> We are led to faith as it is proclaimed in the gospel narrative by prophetical instruments, in that we cannot treat as ambiguous what has been put before us by so many oracles (the prophets). *Sermon* 64.1[58]

In dealing with mankind's human condition, Leo maintained that Adam's fall was occasioned by the temptation of the devil together with man's desire to achieve angelic

[58]SC 74, 85.

honors. He cleverly weaves his doctrine of the fall into the context of the Incarnation.

> Adam neglecting God's command brought in the condemnation of sin. Jesus came under the law to regain liberty for the just. Adam obeying the devil unto prevarication merited that all should die in him. Christ obeying the Father unto the cross brought it about that in him all are revivified. Adam, jealous of the angels' honor, surrendered the dignity of human nature. Christ, taking on the condition of our inferiority because of which he descended into the inferior world, has relocated its inhabitants in heaven.
>
> Christ's redemptive activity was prepared by God in his mercy from the beginning of the universe. In sending his Son as a singular physician for human ills, God enabled him to accomplish what neither the law of Moses nor the prophets could achieve.
>
> The redemption should be realized by an exercise of liberty in keeping with evangelical discipline. It should be exercised by the works of mercy and justice that have been given a special status by Christ enabling the Christian to love what God loves and avoid what displeases God. *Sermon* 25.5[59]

Leo traces the course of the redemption in the faithful's liturgical experience. In baptism, he maintains the contagion of the ancient damnation is expunged so that mankind becomes the body of Christ as Christ is the body of man. Speaking of the lenten fast, he observes:

> At all times and in keeping with both Testaments, God's mercy is sought by means of castigation of one's body and mind. For nothing is more efficacious in beseeching God

[59]SC 49, 134.

> than that a person judge himself and never cease asking forgiveness from God since he knows himself never to be without fault. Human nature has vice in itself, not placed there by the Creator, but contracted through prevarication .... Hence, the interior man, although already regenerated in Christ and liberated from the den of captivity, still has insidious conflicts within the flesh. For when concupiscence is contained, repugnance is experienced. In their discord, it is not easy to achieve a perfect victory. So that the evils that are to be broken off do not harm, and what are to be suppressed, do not wound .... Who is able to so disconnect himself from the pleasures of the body or its pain that he will not experience that which exteriorly either pleases or harms. Joy is indivisible; sorrow all pervasive. *Sermon* 90.1[60]

In governing the Church, Leo set out norms of propriety and moderation. He amalgamated ecclesiastical procedures based on the Scriptures with Roman law putting a juridical structure under the Roman primacy. He maintained that the Church should exercise moderation in its dealings with individuals, whether political officials or the simple faithful. It had to be severe with the obdurate, but quick in offering pardon to the repentent.

His letters deal with moral and spiritual problems such as how to attend the dying when they have lost consciousness; cautioning the bishops of Sicily not to tolerate the custom of public confession in Church lest they give rise to feuds; and counselling what to do about a prisoner of war who returns after seven years (the legal limit before an official declaration of death and the right to remarry) and finds his wife married in good faith to someone else.

> You assert that through the destruction of war and the assult of the enemy, some marriages were destroyed when husbands were carried off into captivity and the wives left behind were deserted. Because they thought their hus-

[60]SC 200, 110-112.

bands were either dead or in perpetual captivity, under the pressure of loneliness, these women married other men. Now the situation has changed for the better ... and some of those thought to be dead have returned ... Now there is doubt as to what should be ordained for these women who married other husbands ... We know it is written that "a woman is joined to a man by God" (Proverbs 19:14) and "what God has joined let no man put asunder" (Matthew 19:6). Hence we believe that the bond of legitimate marriage should be restored ... and each one should get back that which he legally possessed. However, the man who took the place of the husband thought dead is not to be judged guilty nor considered as a usurper of another man's right. Many things belonging to those who were led into captivity could pass into the possession of another. Yet it is absolutely just that on their return these men have restored to them what was theirs. *Letter* 159, 1[61]

In the end he seems to give the returning prisoner a choice; either to repossess his wife or to let her live in peace with his surrogate.

In keeping with the canons of the Holy Fathers, Leo reminds the bishops of the procedures to be observed in selecting bishops.

The procedure to be followed is this ... Even if the people testify to a man's virtuous life, he is not to be chosen if he is a layman, a neophyte, a man married to a second wife, or a man who has but one wife if she is a widow. This choosing of bishops is so important a matter that what is not called a fault for other members of the Church is, nevertheless, to be considered illicit for them.

Although persons outside the clerical state are free to seek after married union, and the procreation of children,

[61]PL 54, 1136.

still in order to exemplify the purity of perfect chastity, carnal marriage is not permitted even to subdeacons, so that those who have wives may be as if they had none, and those who have none may remain single . . . .

When then the selection of the highest priest is being taken care of, let him be preferred above all whom the clerics and people have harmoniously agreed to ask for. But if perhaps some votes come out in favor of another person, then let the one be preferred who, in the judgment of the metropolitan, has greater efforts and merits in his favor. No one of course is to be consecrated without the wishes of the people and their requesting it. Otherwise the citizens will despise or hate the bishop . . . on the grounds that they were not permitted to have the man of their choice. *Epistle* 14, 3-5[62]

Speaking of the manner in which the bishop should correct, Leo says:

Although among our sluggish and negligent brothers there is generally something requiring correction by a stern show of authority, the correction should be applied without destroying charity. Hence, the blessed Apostle Paul instructing Timothy on the government of the Church says: "Do not rebuke an elderly man, but exhort him as you would a father, and young men as brothers." (1 Timothy 5:1-2) *Letter* 14, 1[63]

In calling his vicar in Thessalonica, Bishop Anastasius, to task for overstepping his authority, Leo indulges a rare, personal chagrin.

Although men of priestly rank sometimes do things that are reprehensible, kindness toward those to be corrected

[62]PL 54, 673-674.
[63]PL 54, 669.

is more effective than severity, admonition more than anger, charity more than power. But those who "seek their own interests, not those of Jesus Christ" easily depart from this rule. And while they exult more in dominating than in taking counsel for their subjects, honor puffs up pride, and what was counted on to effect harmony tends to do harm. It is with no small anguish of mind that we have to speak thus. I feel that I myself am somehow involved in blame when I realize that you have unduly departed from the instructions given you. If you had small concern for your own reputation, you should at least have spared mine, so that what you did only according to your own likes might not seem done though a decision of ours. *Epistle* 14, 1[64]

Leo deals with specific situations called to his attention by bishops burdened with pastoral cares. His solutions to problems display the equity and balance of the Roman mind.

No Christian should be excommunicated lightly, nor should this be done at the whim of an angry bishop. It is a penalty which a thoughtful judge should administer unwillingly and, as it were, with sorrow, and in order to punish a serious offense. Now we have discovered that some have been cut off from the grace of membership in the Church for purely trivial acts and statements; and the soul which Christ shed his blood to save, being wounded by the inflicting of so severe a penalty, unarmed, and stripped of all defense, has been subjected to the attacks of the devil so as to be easily overcome. *Epistle* 10, 8[65]

In dealing with the complicated situation caused by the ravages of war and captivity, Leo counsels:

[64]*Ibid.*
[65]PL 54, 635.

Those handmaids of the Lord who lost their perfect
virginity because they were violated by barbarians will be
more praiseworthy in their humility and their feeling of
shame if they do not compare themselves with undefiled
virgins. For although all sin has its source in the will, and
a mind that did not yield could remain uncorrupted by
the pollution of the flesh, it will hinder them less if they
grieve over having lost only in their bodies what they
could not lose in their minds ... It seems best that a
middling course be observed. Let them not be lowered to
the rank of widows, and yet let them not be considered
among the virgins still undefiled. But if they persevere in
the character of virginity, and if they retain in their minds
the resoluteness of chastity, then they are not to be denied
participation in the sacraments. For it is unfair that they
should be branded or accused for losing what hostile
force took away, not something they lost of their own free
will. *Epistle* 12, 11[66]

In keeping with both Jewish and Christian tradition, Leo
condemned usury outright.

This matter also in our opinion ought not to be passed
over in silence. Certain people, ensnared by greed for
base gain, are letting out money at interest and seeking to
grow rich from the returns. We grieve that this occurs not
only among those holding office among the clergy but
also among the laity who wish to go by the name of
Christian. We order that those convicted of this be
severely punished, so as to remove every occasion of sin.
Epistle 4[67]

In his overall attitude, despite the legalistic turn of his
education and vocabulary, Leo personifies moderation in
his moral and ethical admonitions:

[66]PL 54, 655.
[67]PL 54, 613.

Just as there are certain matters that cannot be changed by any consideration, so there are many that require compromise because of age or as demanded by circumstance .... In dubious or obscure matters, a course is to be followed which is not contrary to the Gospel precepts or the decrees of the Holy Fathers. *Letter* 167, 3[68]

In his ecclesial construct, Leo maintains that in the Body of Christ sanctified by the Holy Spirit, the members are held together by a *consortium gratiae* (a gathering of grace), excluding those who will not accept its belief and practice.

It is the Holy Spirit who instructs in the Scriptures and although frequently the mystery of the message is difficult to understand, there is never need for doubt. Even the attack of heretics can render faith clearer and stronger through the assistance given to the faithful by the Holy Spirit in overcoming difficulties. *Letter* 102.1[69]

While Leo amalgamated Roman law with the law of Christ, his greatness resides in his doctrinal insistence on the mystery involved in Christ and in the supernatural charisms of a life pursued by man in Christ's body, the Church.

Pope Gregory I (590-604)

Amid the clash of empires at the dawn of the Middle Ages, Pope Gregory I set about creating a new pastoral theology. His accomplishment was to serve western society well down to the Carolingian renewal in the ninth century and the intellectual renaissance of the twelfth.

Born of a Christian patrician family — two of his ancestors had been popes — Gregory was educated to the law and served both as prefect of the city of Rome and as the pope's ambassador in Constantinople. There he preached a series of homilies on the Book of Job that were eventually turned

[68]PL 54, 1202.
[69]PL 54, 985.

into his *Moralia*. An assiduous preacher as bishop of Rome, his homilies on the Gospels, on the prophet Ezekiel, and on the Canticle of Canticles were fleshed out into the teachings of his *Pastoral Care*, a manual for bishops dealing with the moral and doctrinal needs of the faithful. His four Books of Dialogues on the miracles of the Italian saints is "the *City of God* rewritten for the untrained."

In the introduction to his *Moralia*, Gregory confessed:

> Indefinitely for a long time I put off the grace of conversion. Even after experiencing the desire for heaven, I felt it preferable to retain the habits of the world. From that time, it seemed to me that what I desired was eternal love. But the fetters of enrooted habits kept me from changing my way of life. My spirit forced me not to serve the world except in appearance. But solicitude for this world brought a thousand cares contrary to my own desires that retained me not only in appearance but much worse within my soul. *Letter to St. Leander*[70]

Gregory's moral teaching is anchored on man's fundamental weakness due to original sin. In simple terms he depicts the first man and woman as the object of Satan's envy due to the immortality with which they were created.

Gregory traces the devil's success to three vices. He sees the root of sinfulness as pride, avarice and the desire to achieve godliness not by virtue but by stealth. In depicting the fall of mankind, he follows the text of Genesis literally without the historico-mystical observations of Augustine. Concentrating on Adam as representative of the human species, he elucidates the elements of the temptation as threefold.

> The ancient enemy attacked our first parent with three temptations, namely gluttony, vain glory and avarice ... He tempted with gluttony when he proffered the forbidden fruit of the tree and persuaded him to eat; he tempted him with vain glory when he said they would

know good from evil. Avarice is not only the desire for money, but also for honor. Hence when one seeks after honor beyond what is proper, this is rightly called avarice ... They had truly been made to live in freedom, but through covetousness in evil they became liable to death. *Homily in Evang.* 16.2[71]

Gregory next embarks on a psychological explanation of the process whereby Satan succeeds.

The devil taking us over in the guise of our first parent, as it were, justly held mankind in captivity. For endowed with free will, mankind consented to his persuasion to injustice .... In four steps the evil was perpetrated ... by suggestion, selection, consent and the audacity of self-defense. The serpent suggested. Eve was pleased. Adam consented and did not, through audacity, want to admit his fault when called into question. *Moralia* 17.30.46[72]

Gregory further elucidates the process of conscience.

By the law of nature mankind is forced to know whether what he does is good or evil. Else how is he liable to judgment if he is not able to know what he is doing. Thus even they who refuse to study the commandments of the Lord know whether what they are doing is good or evil. For if they do not know what they are doing why do they boast about their other deeds. Again, if they do not know when they are doing wrong, why do they avoid the eyes of others doing the same thing? Because they know that what they are doing is wrong, they do not want to be seen by others. If indeed they do not truly think they are doing wrong they would not fear to be seen by others. But as they know they are doing wrong, they have their conscience as witness, and their reason as judge. *Moralia* 27.25.48[73]

[71]PL 76, 1136.
[72]PL 76, 32.
[73]PL 76, 427.

Gregory claims that through sin the will has been weakened. Without expressly treating the problem, he follows the Council of Orange (525) in his conviction that mankind retains the ability to choose between good and evil.

This freedom is made possible by grace.

> With God's grace given us beforehand our free will follows in doing good, and we say we are free, when we consent to the Lord who frees us. *Moralia* 24.10.24[74]

Gregory sees the transmission of original sin as somehow connected with sexual concupiscence and the conjugal act of procreation.

> While we have become holy we were not born holy for we are all contaminated by the condition of our corruptible nature as the prophet proclaims: "Behold I was conceived in iniquity and my mother begot me in evil doing" (Psalm 50:7). He alone was born holy who conquered that condition in our sinful nature, who was not conceived from the mixture of a carnal union. *Moralia* 18.52.84[75]

Nevertheless, Gregory wishes to portray marriage as good and unobjectionable.

> We do not say that marriage is sinful ... But because the licit union of the couple cannot be without the pleasure of the flesh they must abstain from entering the sacred place since their voluptuousness cannot be without fault. *Epistle Bk* 11, 64[76]

Gregory experiences great difficulty in explaining how the soul, created by God and therefore good, comes into the world stained with original sin.

> If the soul is not born with the flesh, why is it bound with sin in that flesh which comes forth from Adam? If the

[74]PL 76, 299.
[75]PL 76, 89.
[76]PL 77, 1196.

body is tainted with the original fault, how is the soul given by God guilty, since it had not yet consented to the actual delict with the body?

Why therefore is an infant who has done nothing not pure in the sight of Almighty God? Why unless cleansed in baptism with water, is it not clean? Why do all men die in Adam, if not bound by the bond of original sin? *Epistle Bk* 9, 52[77]

He gives up saying; "In this life the problem is insolvable."

Evil indeed is without substance. Whatever is, has about it the nature of goodness.

As the abyss is without limits, so sinfulness has no foundation; it is without a proper nature. *Moralia* 6.37.68[78]

Gregory centers on repentance for sin. Penance must be willingly accepted and in keeping with the vigor of the sin committed.

A true Roman to the last, he sees absolute justice prevailing in the final judgment. God can be merciful until death; thereafter, his justice will prevail. Unrepented and unpunished sins will properly merit eternal punishment.

Gregory used his own experience and knowledge of mankind to construct a moral theology finely blended with a psychological appreciation of human virtues and vices. Gifted with unwonted insight he penetrated the depths of human consciousness and caught the foibles and idiosyncrasies of the most foolhardy and meretricious personalities. In his letters and moral treatises, he employs this keen insight and impeccable candor in deciphering the ills and accomplishments of human activity under God's grace and Christ's inspiration. Of two things he is certain, without perseverent grace there is no virtue; and to the deeper mysteries of human nature there are no answers this side of eternity.

[77]PL 77, 990.

[78]PL 76, 388.

Subject Index